GOD AND MYSELF

AN INQUIRY INTO THE TRUE RELIGION

BY

MARTIN J. SCOTT

Published by Left of Brain Books

ISBN 978-1-396-32243-3

First Edition

Table of Contents

PREFACE 1

INTRODUCTION 2

PART I. AN INQUIRY INTO THE TRUE RELIGION 5

CHAPTER I. World Calamities and Providence 5

CHAPTER II. All Thinkers Concerned about Religion 8

CHAPTER III. Men of Great Intelligence Differ 9

CHAPTER IV. The World Manifests a Creator and Ruler 10

CHAPTER V. The Spirituality of The Soul 12

CHAPTER VI. The Immortality of the Soul 14

CHAPTER VII. The Creator and Mankind 17

CHAPTER VIII. Jesus Christ 20

CHAPTER IX. One True Religion 24

CHAPTER X. The True Religion 26

CHAPTER XI. How So Many are in Error 32

CHAPTER XII. How So Many are Indifferent 36

CHAPTER XIII. Rationalism and Materialism 37

CHAPTER XIV. Accusations against the True Church 41

CHAPTER XV. Attitude of the True Believer 47

PART II. THE PRINCIPAL TEACHING OF THE CATHOLIC CHURCH 50

CHAPTER I. Why there are Mysteries in Religion 50

CHAPTER II. The Trinity 52

CHAPTER III. The Incarnation 54

CHAPTER IV. The Redemption 56

CHAPTER V. The Mother of God 58

CHAPTER VI. The Head of the Church 60
CHAPTER VII. The Bible 63
CHAPTER VIII. Hell 66
CHAPTER IX. The Sacraments 68
CHAPTER X. The Eucharist 70
CHAPTER XI. The Mass 73
CHAPTER XII. Confession 75
CHAPTER XIII. Marriage 77
CHAPTER XIV. Prayer 80
A LIST OF BOOKS 82

PREFACE

THIS is a little book for those seeking a right understanding of the true religion. It is written in a simple and, it is hoped, friendly manner. It is an attempt to look at things in the ordinary common-sense way. The religion of God is for all people. It should appeal to the simple as well as to the learned. In these days, even learned people are too busy to read long or learned treatises. This is short. It is not written in a theological way, but as a plain statement, which it is hoped will carry conviction. It takes nothing for granted. It begins with the beginning. Although it deals with the sublimest matters that can affect mankind, there is an endeavor to use the simplest language. I have tried to get away from a bookish way of talking and to deal with the matter as men in the street deal with the problems that confront them.

For close on to twenty years I have been in touch with men and women who were agitated by the things here presented. To every thinking person, these subjects must from time to time rise up and claim attention. The world is now deeply stirred. The best established things are being tested. The past few years have seen many isms collapse. Religion itself has been challenged. This little treatise is a reply. It will also help those already instructed to meet the difficulties of the day better. Moreover, it will be of especial benefit to those who are engaged in giving instruction to seekers after the truth. By reading this book through carefully, an inquirer will be informed on all the main points of the true religion. As a handbook for inquirers, it aims at seeing things from their standpoint. In this way, it is hoped that they in turn will be led to see the true religion as it is. For to see it as it is will surely lead to its acceptance. Misrepresentation and misunderstanding are the two great sources of error. To remove these and in so doing to set forth the splendor of truth is the purpose of these pages.

INTRODUCTION

THE condition of the world to-day makes men serious-minded. The greater part of mankind is suffering, making enormous sacrifices, some of life and limb, others of relatives, friends, comfort, and even the necessaries of life. People naturally reflect on the purpose of life when they see it spent thus. The pagan motto "eat, drink, and be merry, for to-morrow we die," may be very well when we have youth and pleasure and prosperity, but in times of sacrifice it finds no echo in the heart.

Individuals as well as nations have their periods of sacrifice. Indeed, looking at life broadly, is not every life a sacrifice? If one dies in youth, what a sacrifice of hopes and ambitions! If one lives on to old age, it is only to await some disease or accident as an exit from the stage of life. And the years between, what a conflict they record! Truly, as Scripture tells us, man's life on earth is a warfare. But war has a purpose, a goal. And what is that purpose, that goal?

Down the ages philosophers and sages have essayed to reply, but the only reply that answers the whole call of life is that given by Jesus Christ. Christ changed the face of the earth. The kingdom He founded is now spread over the entire world, and, after a duration of two thousand years, it is the most vigorous in the world to-day. It has passed through worse crises than we behold at present, and after each it has stood erect, stronger than before. Let us go to Christ, therefore, and see what solution He gives to the problem of life.

In his treatise "God and Myself" (An Inquiry into the True Religion), Father Scott presents the religion of Jesus Christ to the ordinary reader in a brief, clear, and most convincing manner. Realizing that misunderstanding is mainly accountable for the sad religious condition of the times, the author has set himself to remove it. This he does by a most lucid statement of the chief points of the Christian religion. In the course of the work the great problems of life which at times confront every individual are clearly stated and as clearly solved. In a word, this treatise enables the average person to give a reason for the faith that is in him, and puts his religious belief on a foundation which nothing can shake. Indeed as a book to inform Catholics thoroughly, and also to give to non-Catholics a right view of the Church, I commend it most highly.

I trust that this volume will go forth as a missioner, and bring firm faith and true comfort to countless souls. Jesus Christ has said: "I am the Light of the world;" Father Scott's book should point the way for many to that Light, which leads infallibly those who follow it. "He that followeth Me walketh not in darkness, but shall have the light of life." Now, more than ever, we need that light.

✠ James Card. Gibbons.

My life is but a weaving
Between my God and me;
I may but choose the colors—
He worketh steadily.
Full oft He weaveth sorrow,
And I, in foolish pride,
Forget He sees the upper
And I the under side.

—FATHER TABB

PART I.

AN INQUIRY INTO THE TRUE RELIGION

CHAPTER I.

World Calamities and Providence

AT certain periods of the world's history men are inclined to ask themselves "Is there any Power on high that cares for human welfare?" Earthquakes, famines, wars, how they work havoc with mankind! If there is a Ruler of the world, why does He allow the dreadful occurrences which at times plunge individuals and whole peoples into misery! Presuming that there is an all-powerful Ruler of the world, how can He be just and wise in view of what we see about us? This reflection comes to every man in moments of affliction, especially if he is the victim of injustice.

Religion has been driven out of the heart of many a man because of injustice and suffering. Injustice there is in the world and suffering and distress. How is it all compatible with government from on high? These are all fair questions which any man, no matter how good he be, may ask.

In our Revolutionary War Washington held his troops at Valley Forge during a very severe winter, although it caused them the most extreme suffering. Half-clad, half-starved, he nevertheless obliged them to continue on. Was Washington unmindful of his men? Who would entertain the thought?

In our Civil War there was a stubborn and bloody fight known as "The Battle of the Wilderness." General Grant, the Commander of the forces of the North, sent regiment after regiment against the death-dealing defences of the enemy. The slaughter was so dreadful that it was called a shambles. But Grant kept it up, day after day. Was General Grant a cruel man? On the contrary, he was so considerate and kind-hearted that he refused to take the sword of Lee on the latter's surrender, and, moreover, the first thing he did after victory was to send rations to the hungry soldiers who had been fighting against him.

Now of course you will say that there is no comparison, that the Ruler of the world is supposed to be all-powerful, while these men had to do the best they could under great limitations. Granted; but at least you will admit, that under certain circumstances a kind person may cause suffering.

Now the point is this, are there any circumstances which will justify a wise and kind Ruler of the world to allow such sufferings as we see in the world? I say that there must be, for the simple reason that He allows them. Hold now, do not say I am begging the question. I am going to assert nothing without demonstration. I say, then, that because the Ruler of the world allows certain shocking things there are circumstances which justify it.

If a Hottentot who never heard anything about dentistry were to see an American mother holding her struggling child while a man with a wrench was pulling its tooth, would he not say: "What a cruel mother!" Of course after explaining the circumstances and showing him the beneficial purpose of the performance he would change his mind. Is it not wise to suppose that when we see things as the Ruler of the world does we should change our minds too? A Hottentot is much better qualified to understand the wisest man in the world than the wisest of mankind is to comprehend the Ruler of the universe.

Some years ago the steamer *General Slocum* caught fire in the East River, New York. It was a Sunday-School excursion on its way to the Sound. Some women, to save their children from the flames, threw them overboard. Suppose you saw only the mother and child and did not know the ship was afire, you would say she was crazy or cruel. We see but a tiny bit of the world-ship. Our whole earth is but a microscopic speck compared to the universe. But, you will say, at least we have ideas of justice, no matter how minute the matter may be, and so we are qualified to pass judgment. Not until you know how that minute particle stands in relation to the rest.

Suppose you saw the wife and children of a condemned man crying and begging the Governor for his pardon, and he refused their supplication, although he had it in his power to grant the pardon, would you call him hard-hearted? Not until you knew the circumstances. He had to consider not only the wife and mother and those children, but the lives of millions in the state he was ruling. Very true, you may rejoin, but the Ruler of the world is presumed to be all-wise as well as all-powerful, and if He is kind and good and just, He should be able to devise ways and means for our welfare which would save us from the suffering and misery which abound. To this, I say, it is only right to suppose that the power and wisdom which created the universe knows how to run it.

When we were children, how we liked to play and how we hated everything that interfered with our pleasures! We found our school tasks disagreeable and often tried to shirk them. Suppose we had asked our parents to let us play instead of making us learn to read and write and figure; should we not curse them in our maturity if they had done as we desired? They looked ahead and realized that to face life without education was too big a price to pay for passing enjoyment.

In comparison with the Ruler of the world the wisest of mankind is less than a little child in the arms of its mother. It is our part to do our duty, and to trust the Creator to do His. All our sense of kindness, mercy, and justice comes from our Maker. The rays from the sun give light and heat, but they are not brighter or warmer than the sun itself. But, you may object, are we not to inquire, to investigate, to solve, or try to solve the problems of life? Certainly. But we come to a point at last where we find that our reason cannot penetrate, and here religion steps in and gives us the solution.

Ex-Ambassador Bryce recently said, "The mists that hang around man's origin and destiny are just as deep as ever they were." His inquiring mind could not penetrate that mist, nor has it ever been penetrated by man. Professor Harnack, one of the greatest Rationalist philosophers of the age, stated in a lecture to university graduates that "Pure knowledge is a glorious thing and woe to the man who holds it light or blunts his sense for it. But to the question whence, whither, and to what purpose are we? it gives an answer to-day as little as it did two or three thousand years ago. Gentlemen, it is religion, the love of God and neighbors, which gives life a meaning. Knowledge cannot do it."

This religion I present to you in the following pages. I promise you that if you read this book carefully, you will have not only a solution, but *the* solution. Only approach the matter with a clear, open mind, I beg of you. The truth asks no favors, all it demands is fairness. Try to give the matter the same candid consideration you do the events of daily life. That is not asking too much, I hope.

CHAPTER II.

ALL THINKERS CONCERNED ABOUT RELIGION

THE most serious thought of the world has been given to religion. The greatest geniuses of all nations have bestowed their best efforts on it. From the time of Jesus Christ to the present day, the literature of the world has given first place to religious topics.

At the very outset I have mentioned Jesus Christ. Do not infer, however, that I take for granted anything about Him. I shall later consider His personality. In fact, Christ is the basis of the Christian religion and everything depends on who and what He is. In these preliminary remarks, I speak in the traditional way, putting the subject before you as millions view it.

You, too, no matter how busy you are, nor how great or little you may be, should give religion consideration. Not to do so is to reject what has most concerned humanity all the ages. If at present there is a wave of indifference abroad, do not be caught in it. Be concerned about what Jesus Christ came from heaven to bring us, what millions of the best men and women have died for, what hundreds of millions are living for, what holds up to mortal men immortality, what places before mankind ideals which are heaven-born and whose adoption will make you a dweller forever in heaven. Be not indifferent to such a boon.

If a worldly prospect promises much or its rejection threatens disaster, men are not indifferent to it. Religion promises eternity of happiness to those who live by it, and threatens eternity of misery to those who reject it. Can you afford to take a chance when so much is at stake?

CHAPTER III.

Men of Great Intelligence Differ

THE first thing that strikes an inquirer after religious truth is that there is such a difference of belief in regard to it. Some claim one religion is true, some another; some reject religion altogether. What is one to do?

When Columbus affirmed that the world was round, some said it was impossible, some believed, some wondered. But the world's roundness did not depend on these beliefs. The world's roundness was a fact. Is religion a fact? If so, we must not be surprised that there are differences of opinion about it. There is hardly a fact in history during the past two thousand years that has not been subject to various and often opposite opinions. Every war is the result of different judgments of a fact. The divergence of religious beliefs shows that religion at all events is a reality. Men do not contend over nothing.

Now this reality, this religion, is it something we can be certain about? May we know its truth, or must we be left groping? Why, if religion is vital, should not God make its truth clear beyond doubt? He has done so. Follow me, and you will see that God has done His part. The rest remains with us. God is the Light amidst darkness. If men will close out the light, He will let them, for He respects our liberty. He wants our free service. He will not force us.

Come with me, then, and see all He has done to establish His religion, to make it evident, to win you and me to loving service here and to eternal enjoyment hereafter. To those who receive Him He gives the power to become the children of God!

CHAPTER IV.

THE WORLD MANIFESTS A CREATOR AND RULER

IN order to lay a solid foundation for our inquiry into the true religion, we shall begin with the existence of God.

By the word God we mean the First Cause of all things. Nothing happens of itself. Everything is caused by something preceding it. But we cannot go back forever,—we must stop somewhere. When we get back to the stopping-point we meet the Cause of all. This we call the First Cause. Since it causes everything else and itself was not caused, it has in itself its own existence necessarily. Now we shall show that this First Cause is personal, an infinitely intelligent and powerful Being.

If we look at a watch and observe its wonderful mechanism and unity of design, we say that its maker is a person of intelligence and skill. Now if we can point to something that shows infinite power and intelligence, we may say that it calls for an infinitely powerful and intelligent maker. Let us consider the world.

The earth turns upon its axis once in twenty-four hours. In so doing it shows the expenditure of great energy. The sun, whose limitless energy confounds calculation, shines in the heavens. Moreover, the earth travels in its orbit, causing the changing seasons, a further demonstration of immeasurable energy. On a starry night the eye searches great distances and beholds the constellations, the planets, and the whole solar system moving around the sun, to say nothing of the mysteries of the infinite beyond. Truly limitless energy with its effects is plainly visible.

Furthermore, note that the great machine of the universe is running on time, even to the second. Our finest watches are but a feeble imitation of the world clock. Our most correct time is taken at the Observatory of Washington. Every day at noon the astronomer there times his chronometer by the firmament, and then by telegraph sends the true time throughout the country. We regulate our watches by the world clock.

What is the best human timepiece compared with the wonderful mechanism of the universe, so infallible, so reliable throughout the years, in fact throughout all the centuries? Here we have infinite energy with unvarying precision plainly visible. Now let us analyze this. Man has never been able to create a single foot-pound of force. With coal and water power, steam and electricity, he can transform force, but he cannot make it. The power to make force exists above the possibilities of man,—it is a creative act demanding infinite power.

There is no bridge between nothing and something; such a chaos is spanned only by infinitude. The First Cause of force in its various manifestations is the Creator. That Creator is not only the Architect of the universe, but He maintains its infinite machinery in marvellous motion and accuracy. The greatest piece of mechanism, the most stupendous feat of engineering, the sublime mystery of world dynamics, the infinitude of the firmament, demonstrate a Creator and Ruler of the world, an intelligent and personal God.

CHAPTER V.

The Spirituality of The Soul

WE have seen that there is an intelligent and personal God who is the Creator and Ruler of the world. Let us now consider man, for religion means the bond between man and God.

Man is a creature, first of all, with understanding. Mere matter does not understand, so man is more than matter.

Man is also a creature with free will. He can say yes or no, and no one can force him against his will. Mere matter does not determine itself, so man is more than matter.

Man is capable of generalizing, or rising in thought above what his senses perceive. For example, he has ideas of the following things which do not exist in themselves: *endlessness, nothing, future, abstract.* No one ever saw an abstraction, yet man knows the meaning of abstract. No one ever saw nothing or felt it, or realized it by any of the senses, yet the mind knows what *nothing* means, has an idea of *nothing*. Matter cannot abstract and generalize and compare, so again man is more than matter.

There is a power in man which commands his body, forces it to do what he wishes, even forces himself to do what he shrinks from. A man may feel tired, his body may be fatigued, his limbs may be sore and injured, but he can compel his tired body to work on. Mere matter cannot command, so man is more than matter.

Man can originate and compose. The poet gives us lofty ideas, the musician creates marvellous harmonies and melodies, the workman invents new devices. Mere matter cannot thus soar aloft and penetrate into the realms of possibility.

As you read these lines, you are doing your own thinking, and as a result you may alter your plan of life. Matter cannot estimate and decide, so man is more than matter.

That power in man which is not matter we call spirit. Man is therefore a spiritual being, made up of matter and spirit. Religion means the bringing of our spirit into right relation with the Creator. Religion has no connection with matter or animals because they cannot comprehend. God made them as they are, and they are incapable of doing otherwise than as determined.

Matter is subject to fixed laws which no power on earth can change; animals are subject to fixed laws, called instinct, which nothing can change. You can teach an animal a few tricks by force of training, but this is merely artificial, like painting wood to resemble oak. But man is independent; he can do as he likes; he comprehends; he is the only creature who can defy law; he can use his liberty even against his own good. A drunkard, a gambler, a libertine, may know that he is bringing disease and death on himself, but he may go ahead. Man can even defy God himself. And he does. That makes sin, when a man deliberately does what he knows is wrong.

Religion then means bringing man into harmony with God, bringing him into God's way of living, bringing him back to what is right. Man has a tendency to be a law unto himself, to do as he likes. But God gave man liberty to serve Him, to do His will. He could have made man like the rest of nature, subject to fixed laws, but He did not. He made him free to give him the opportunity of showing loyalty and allegiance to Him who so wonderfully made him.

God's law obliges man to direct his life to please God and not to suit himself, and yet we see many people living just to suit themselves. But is God to be trifled with? We must obey the laws of our country. How about God's laws, which are more sacred? Because God is good and patient and does not punish instantly, it does not follow that man can go on sinning.

For after death, the judgment!

We shall next consider the immortality of the soul.

CHAPTER VI.

The Immortality of the Soul

THERE is a God, the Creator and Ruler of the world. He gave laws to all creation. Every scientist knows that. Every creature except man is governed by fixed laws. The stars, the planets, the air, the chemical elements, plants, water, animals, birds,—all these are so governed by laws, or instinct, that you can foretell their action under given conditions. But man has no fixed rule of action.

You can never tell what a man may decide on. You may guess, but it is merely a guess. He may be surrounded by evil and yet be good; on the other hand, he may be under good influences and yet do evil. He may plan for the future, or he may think only of the present; he may prefer to die rather than be a coward, or he may not care whether he is considered a coward or a knave; some men prefer honor to life, others sacrifice honor for a trifle; a man may be dying of hunger and refuse to take bread at the price of sin, another might sin for a trifle; the same man to-day may be an angel, to-morrow a devil; a man may keep a law or break it, whether it be a law of health, country, or God. In a word, a man is free to do right or wrong.

In giving him this great power, did the Creator intend to let him use it without accountability? If the Creator gives man a law, is He indifferent as to whether man observes the law or not? If man breaks the laws of right and justice which are in his very nature, does the Author of nature not care? Did the Creator give laws to be broken? All this leads up to the question of the immortality of the soul.

If you break a law of health, you suffer for it. If you violate your country's law, you are punished. If you violate God's law, what? We know that clever men can be dishonest and escape detection, and profit by their dishonesty. Can they cheat the Creator and Ruler of the world? Yet they seem to. Monuments have been raised to men who were scoundrels, great orations have been pronounced over men who were iniquitous. Either there is another life where God rewards the good and punishes the wicked, or else we must conclude that he who breaks the law can laugh at the Lawgiver.

Unless man lives on after death, God cares as much for those who are disloyal to Him as for those who are loyal. Unless man is immortal, the Creator made wise laws and yet cares not if they are observed. But as God is wise and just and all-powerful, He would be stultifying Himself if He made laws not to be observed.

The conclusion then is plain. Since the good are not always rewarded here nor the wicked always punished, there is a hereafter where justice is done to all. This is a moral argument based on the fitness of things. We shall now give a scientific proof of the immortality of the soul.

Matter never perishes, but merely changes. For instance, wood does not cease to exist when it is burned, but is changed into ashes, smoke, etc. The ashes and smoke again resolve themselves into other elements, and so on indefinitely. This is scientifically called the indestructibility of matter. Matter changes by being broken up into its component parts. When it can be no more resolved into parts, it forms other combinations and continues on as another substance.

The soul is spiritual. It has no parts, it cannot be divided; hence it cannot be destroyed, it cannot perish; by its very nature it will last forever, it is immortal.

I may add another proof. Every nation, civilized, or barbarous, or savage, believes in a future state. This universal belief must have a foundation in nature, since it is as extensive as humanity. The Creator is therefore its author, and it is consequently true. Moreover, there is something in each one of us that tells us that we shall not end forever. Every man at special periods feels this. All nature seems to proclaim it. The trees blooming after the dead winter, the grain of corn rotted in the soil springing to new life, the base caterpillar feeding on the earth coming forth from its tomb as the beautiful butterfly,—all symbolize the life after death.

Man, the lord of creation, has certainly a nobler destiny than the things he dominates. The mind of man that penetrates in thought the very heavens and sees the almighty hand that framed the universe has certainly a career beyond the earth he treads on. The Creator did not put hopes in the human breast merely to mislead men, but to be a guiding star to higher and nobler things; yea, to lead man back to the very Author of his being. The Creator is the Alpha and Omega, the beginning and the end.

I have brought to your consideration the spirituality and immortality of the soul because nowadays materialism is a reigning cult. Materialists proclaim that everything is matter, and that consequently we need give no thought to religion, which concerns the spirit.

Man likes to have his own way, to be his own master; he dislikes to be enlightened if it is going to curtail his liberty. He listens eagerly to a cult that flatters him and leaves him great latitude. If the true religion allowed man the license that the various cults and isms give him, there is no one in the world who would not see the truth of it and embrace it.

CHAPTER VII.

THE CREATOR AND MANKIND

IT has been demonstrated in the preceding pages that the Maker of all things imposed His will on them. In the firmament and in the elements of earth this will is expressed in what we call nature's laws. They are inflexible. In animals it is instinct which governs invariably. But what rules man? Conscience. This is God's will conveyed to man, telling him to do right and to avoid wrong.

As an example of how conscience acts, take a child who tells his first lie. When for the first time he says what he knows is not so, a blush comes to his countenance. This blush is the external sign of the shock within as nature cries out against falsehood. A confirmed liar shows no external disturbance because he has silenced conscience. Some nations and some individuals have more delicate consciences than others, but there are certain fundamental things which every people and every person feel to be obligatory.

Conscience is the bond between the Creator and the creature. And just as an individual may by carelessness or selfishness or licentiousness distort or destroy conscience, so may nations. We have an instance of this in the degraded and unblushing immorality of ancient Rome, even at the very height of her civilization. But the Creator has nevertheless asserted Himself. Nation after nation that has turned from righteousness has come to a sad end.

And so with the individual. He who sows the wind reaps the whirlwind. Often, however, the wicked prosper and the just suffer, but this is because God, if He always rewarded the good and punished the wicked here below, would be a mere employer, not the Lord and Creator. God could stop all the evil in the world instantly if He wished to, but He would then be interfering with the free will He has bestowed on man. For if He punished transgressions of His law on the spot, man would be morally forced to keep it and could give no external manifestation of his submission and loyalty.

So God permits evil in order to leave man free to choose between good and evil. For if there were no evil in the world, man would have no exercise of his liberty, which consists in absolute freedom of choice. If a man could only do right, he would be bound, not free.

Now with liberty goes responsibility. Man must answer for the use he makes of his wondrous gift. This brings him in direct relation with his Maker. The greatest transgressions may be those unseen by one's fellow-man. God alone knows all and sees all. Hence the necessity of a guiding code of morals by which man will be judged. This code is written on the heart of man. It was also given on Mt. Sinai in the Ten Commandments. Even apart from Mt. Sinai's promulgation, is there any one of the Ten Commandments that any decent man would wish to see revoked? Would you respect God if He permitted lying, or stealing, or dishonor to parents, or the lust that would rob you of your wife's affection or your daughter of her virtue? Would you respect God if He did not demand your reverence and obedience?

If God is entitled to our obedience, He is bound to make known to us His law. He might do this in various ways. It is not for us to say how He shall do it. He could command us directly and personally, He could do it by the ministry of angels, He could write His law in the firmament so that all might read it. But He has not chosen to do so. Instead He has made a covenant with mankind, employing human agencies to make known His dispensations. This is a statement. It requires proof, which we shall proceed to give shortly.

The covenant between God and man is called religion. Religion comes from the two Latin words *re* and *ligo*, which mean to bind back. It signifies the bond by which man is brought back into right relations with God. We, like sheep, had gone astray; individuals and nations had departed from right. God would bring back His erring children, and the ordinary means is by religion. This bond between the Creator and His creature we shall now consider.

I ask you to take up the matter in a fair way, as far as possible without prejudice. Prejudice kills right judgment. In a law suit, see how each party misjudges the other. That is why they must appear before a judge, who hears both sides. In our Civil War see how the North viewed the South and the South the North.

A person who is not a Christian, with difficulty views the Church rightly. Among Christians behold how one sect regards another, and, above all, see how the sects regard the Catholic Church. Persons who have joined the Catholic Church from other denominations marvel at the way in which they had misunderstood her. Their first and strongest feeling after conversion is how they could have so mistaken and misrepresented her. As a rule, they burn with zeal to have others see her truth and beauty once they have beheld her as she is.

Christ said, speaking of His Church: "As the world has hated me, so will it hate you." In connection with this saying, I have an occurrence to relate. It is given by the late Father Gallwey, the noted Jesuit. Three English gentlemen, who were very literary, had the custom of meeting at one another's homes in turn and discussing literary topics. They read, each time they met, portions of the great masters,—Homer, Virgil, Horace, Dante, Shakespeare, etc. They always concluded by reading a passage from the Bible, the King James version.

It happened that one day they touched on that part wherein Christ uses the words I referred to: "As the world has hated me, so will it hate you." One of the gentlemen remarked on hearing the phrase that it had a meaning for him which it had never had before. Christ, he said, was here giving a characteristic of His Church,—it was to be hated and persecuted by the world. "Now, my friends," he continued, "which of the Christian churches does the world to-day hate and persecute?"

They went into the matter and concluded that there was but one church in the world with which the world was in opposition, and always had been, the Catholic Church. All the other churches had made friends with the world, were living on good terms with the world. From the Apostles down to the present day, the Catholic Church stood out against the spirit of the world, and the world stood against it.

After these reflections, the three agreed that it was worth while looking into the claims of such a church. They did so, and found to their astonishment that all their lives they were opposed to a church that they did not know. They had taken for granted the statements of her opponents and had arrayed themselves against her. On investigating for themselves, they saw things differently, and were convinced that she was the true Church of Christ. They had the strength of their convictions, for they sought out a priest and applied for admission into the Church. Father Gallwey was the priest and he it is who gives us these particulars.

We shall now, with unprejudiced mind, I trust, consider the matter of religion and its relation to ourselves personally. Please leave others out of the question and reflect on the points which follow as a personal matter between you and your Maker. *God and Myself.*

CHAPTER VIII.

Jesus Christ

ALL very well, you say, but you are supposing that there is a divine religion and that it is yours. Not at all, as you will see. There is no supposition about it. I stated the ideals and hopes of millions merely to show the magnitude and significance of religion, and to have you reflect on whether or not you could afford to ignore what has been vital to so many. But now I ask you to consider the evidence for the divinity of the Christian religion.

Kindly follow my statements as a juror would a witness. If there is absolute evidence and logic, be courageous and give a verdict accordingly. No priest wants to lead an inquirer into his religion except by the light of truth. He would give his very life to bring the religion of Jesus Christ into an other's life, but he would not want anyone to receive that faith unless that one were convinced that it was divine truth.

You will admit that if Jesus Christ is truly God, we can put absolute credence in Him. God can neither deceive nor be deceived. And if, being God, He declares that He established a religion and gives His word that it will be in the world to the end, we can believe that His divine religion is in the world today. That much is clear and no one can or does take exception to it. This is a platform on which all can stand, no matter how broad or narrow they may be.

Now, I am not saying which is the religion of Jesus Christ; that will come later. Here I merely state that if Christ is God and has established a religion to last to the end, it is in the world now. And, in passing, if God saw fit to establish a religion for you, you cannot treat it lightly.

Is Jesus Christ God? A little question, yet fundamental of all Christian belief. What I propose to do is this: To show that Jesus Christ is God, that He founded a divine Church, that He commanded all to enter it, and that each one has his own accountability to God in the matter. This is my program; you know just what is before you; now to proceed.

There has been more literature on the personality of Jesus Christ than on anything else in the world. I might take a dozen different methods of proving the divinity, the real divinity, of Jesus Christ, but, as this is only a short treatise and intended for ordinary inquirers, I select the one which appeals to ordinary common sense, which is, after all, the safest standard.

Jesus was born into this world at the time foretold by the prophecies, in the manner they describe, and in the place specified. His whole life is such a fulfilment of the prophecies that it would seem that they were written after His life rather than hundreds of years before.

He predicted definitely His own passion and death and resurrection.

His whole life is pronounced by all classes of men the most perfect ever lived. He did the works which only a divine power could do and pointed to them as evidence of His divinity. He gave sight to the blind, cleansed the leper made the cripple walk, calmed the angry elements, raised the dead to life.

He repeatedly declared that He was the true Son of God, one in nature with the Father, and, in the end, He died for publicly declaring before the highest tribunal of Israel that He was God. The Jews understood Him to mean God in the real, true sense, for otherwise they would not have charged Him with blasphemy and condemned Him to be crucified for making Himself God.

All these facts are recorded in the Bible. Taking the Bible merely as an historical document, it is the best authenticated book in the world. Moreover, the Jews themselves never denied these deeds of Jesus.

Jesus therefore declared on oath before the sacred Tribunal of His own people that He was true God. Are we to believe Him?

All men admit that Christ is the most perfect man that ever lived; now the most perfect man does not deceive; therefore, Christ is God.

But, you will say, perhaps He was under an hallucination. All admit that Jesus is the best balanced personality that the world has known. His character was absolutely poised and judicial and unruffled and masterful. No hallucination there. Since, therefore, Jesus was incapable of falsehood or of hallucination, His word stands. He is God. *Christ is either God or a bad man.*

Furthermore, He had nothing to gain by declaring Himself God. Honors and power He did not want. He knew that declaring Himself God meant an ignominious death, but He so declared Himself. No one, except for truth, speaks the word which takes away life.

And the teaching of Jesus is just what we should expect from one who is divine. The great St. Augustine said that he could not believe Christ was God if His doctrine was conceivable by the human mind. "I believe Christ was

God," he said, "because no human intelligence ever conceived or could conceive what He taught." The Blessed Eucharist, the Trinity, the Incarnation, the Fatherhood of God and the Brotherhood of man, all these are conceptions outside the range of the human intellect.

Moreover, Jesus Christ is the turning-point of history. We date our years before and after Christ. We say an event occurred B.C. (before Christ) or A.D. (after Christ).

Jesus also foretold the dispersion and continuation of the Jewish race. We know how tenacious the Jews were of their religion and their country. The Jews to-day are the only people of the world without a country, king or flag. And they are the most intellectual and prosperous and race-loving people on earth. The most astonishing thing is this: Since the coming of Christ, the Jews have had no Temple, no sacrifice, no High Priest. This is wonderful when we consider their religious tenacity.

Since the destruction of the Temple at Jerusalem, they have had no Temple. Synagogues they have a plenty and rabbis, but no Temple, no sacrificing priesthood, no High Priest. Jesus, the great High Priest, replaced their priesthood, and His Church replaced their Temple.

It may be asked, Why did the Jews not accept Jesus if He proved His claims? The people did accept Him. Behold how they acclaimed Him in the procession of palms. It was because the multitude believed in Jesus that the Scribes and Pharisees said: We must do something; all the people are following after Him. (John xi.) They held a council and decided to kill Christ. (John xii. 9–12.) But the multitude was so attached to Jesus that the leaders were afraid to proceed "lest there should be a tumult among the people."

To-day we see the same thing, in certain quarters, where the will of a few designing men thwarts the will of the people. The acceptance of Christ meant the rejection of the Scribes and Pharisees. They rejected Truth to hold power because they were blinded by passion, as many are to-day.

As the divinity of Jesus Christ is the foundation of the divine Christian religion, I have put it before you in a way which I trust will speak for itself. Once we know that Christ is God, it is our part to accept reverently what He says. We may use all our powers of mind to examine and prove His divinity,—that is the right use of reason,—but once we see that He is God, it is our duty to believe Him.

God does not ask us to understand Him, but to believe Him, to serve Him, and to love Him. We can scarcely understand our fellow-men; how may we hope to comprehend God? He wants us to trust Him, as a child does its mother. He wants us to honor His truthfulness by believing Him simply because He says so. This is the meaning of Faith. There is no faith where you verify and comprehend. You believe two and two make four, not on anyone's word, but because it is evident. You believe the world is round because you can travel round it. But you believe a doctor on faith when he tells you that you have pneumonia, and you take a prescription from a druggist on faith, not because you ascertain it is correct, but because you trust in his knowledge and uprightness. Nearly all human lives are lived largely by trust in one another. God wants us to trust Him!

Realizing that Jesus Christ is God, and that heaven and earth may pass away, but not His word, we shall next consider if He established a religion in the world and gave it a character by which we may readily know it.

CHAPTER IX.

One True Religion

WE have seen that Jesus Christ is God. He came upon earth and became one of us in order to raise us up from this earth to heaven. God became man that men might become the children of God. How do we know this? From His own words. We have seen that once we believe that Christ is God, we take as true what He declares, so there will be no further argument about His words. We may and should use all the reason God has given us to investigate if He is God, but that once determined, it is the dictate of sound reason to accept without question what He says.

Christ says: "He who follows me shall have a hundredfold and life everlasting; He who loses his life for my sake shall find it; I go to prepare a place for you." To the penitent thief, He said: "This day thou shalt be with me in Paradise." In regard to the multitudes, He said: "Father, I will that where I shall be they also shall be." Finally, hear His words to those who have lived goodly lives: "Come, ye blessed of my Father and possess the kingdom of heaven."

Christ came not merely for the people who lived in His day, but for all nations to the end of the world. But how was He to reach them and minister unto them? He could have done it in various ways, but we must consider, not what He might have done, but what He did. And how did He provide for His ministry to men? He established a Church which was to continue forever the work He began. And how do we know this? From His plain declaration: "Thou art Peter, and upon thee I will build my church." (Matt. xvi. 17–20) "As the Father hath sent me, so I send you." (John xx. 21) "Go ye into the whole world and preach the things I have commanded you, and behold I shall be with you all days to the end of the world." Matt. xxviii. 18–20.) This Church, then, is a teaching body, truly representing Christ on earth. For this reason He gave to His Church all the power of an ambassador: "He who hears you, hears me." "All power is given to me in heaven and on earth." "As the Father hath sent me, so I send you." What Christ is to the eternal Father, the Church is to Christ. The best definition of the Church is to state that it is the continuation of Jesus Christ in the world.

Our divine Lord, having thus established a religion, took good care to guarantee its continuation and absolute truth. Here is His guarantee: "The gates of hell shall not prevail against it; The Spirit of Truth, whom my Father will send, will teach you all truth; I shall be with you all days to the end of the world." Christ cannot be with error; hence, we have here the guarantee of infallibility to His Church. Indeed, how could a representative of God be anything else but truth itself? Christ did not say His Church would not have human frailty; indeed, He foretold that scandals would come; but what He did foretell and guarantee was that it should never teach error.

A judge of a court may not be an impeccable man, but he may be a good judge. A doctor may be subject to illness, but he may nevertheless be an excellent doctor and prescribe beneficially for others. So the Church of God, which is not made up of angels, but of men, may in some of her pastors fail to live up to its own high teaching, but by God's special guarantee, it can never teach what is false.

We have not stated yet what church is the one founded by Christ and guaranteed as His representative. Only this have we declared and demonstrated: that Christ, the Son of God, established a Church, and that He made it His representative among men and guaranteed it against misrepresenting Him.

Next, we shall proceed to find out where that Church is to-day, for we have God's word that it is in the world, and will be unto the end.

CHAPTER X.

THE TRUE RELIGION

NOW we come to a delicate point, delicate because very many who have agreed with all we have hitherto said will here begin to be sensitive and even suspicious. No one readily grants that he is not right. That is why the proud Scribes and Pharisees rejected Jesus. His teaching was not according to their notion. Instead of realizing and confessing that He was God, since He did the works of God, they explained away His deeds, distorted His words and rejected Him. They could not deny His miraculous deeds, but they attributed them to Satan; and when Christ refuted them, although silenced, they would not be convinced.

Evidence is not enough unless the mind that views it is candid. Every day we see people who, with the same facts before them, draw different and contradictory conclusions. The fault is not with the evidence, but with the attitude of the beholder. So I ask you, whoever you be and of whatever religious belief, to look quietly and attentively at the facts I am about to present.

God is not going to ask you about others, but about yourself. *God and Myself.* He is not going to ask of you an account of your ancestors' religion, but of your own. Your opportunities may be different from theirs. He will judge you by your own accountability. If at the time of our Lord people refused to listen to Him and follow Him because they would have to change their views, Christianity never would have existed.

God gives you light even while reading these pages, which makes you a different person with a larger responsibility. People at Jerusalem who heard and saw Jesus were differently judged from those who, living at the same time, neither saw nor heard Him. *God and Myself.*

I ask you to consider calmly the things I am now to say, and to be guided by the light of truth, not by the darkness of prejudice. It makes no difference to me personally what effect my words may have on you. All I seek is to do good, to please my Master, God, and to do you a service by making you dearer to God. If there is any personal element in what I am doing, it is the joy which the follower of Christ has in bringing into a human soul the light and peace which He came to impart. As Christ gave His life for His religion, so His minister will give his life, if necessary, to extend that religion, and this because he knows that what Christ says is so: "What doth it profit a man if he gain the whole world and lose his soul?" *God and Myself.*

Which is the divine religion established by Jesus Christ? Is there one, or are there many such? Are there several religions which may equally be the Church of Christ? We have among us Episcopalians, Presbyterians, Baptists, Methodists, Lutherans, Catholics. Are they all right? Are they all wrong?

I must confess that to me it is painful to see so many claimants. I know so many people of different denominations whom I esteem that I hate to believe that their belief is not right. Here let me say a very important thing. In considering this matter, we must distinguish between the man and his creed. A man may be personally sincere, yet his religion may be wrong; in condemning his religion, we do not condemn him. On the other hand, his religion may be true, yet he may be personally a very bad man.

We see this in various other matters. For instance, in politics, a Republican may denounce the Democratic party, yet esteem the individual Democrat. I know a Democrat who spent most of his energy denouncing Republicans, yet his own son and his best friends were Republicans. You may condemn suffragettism, yet admire and esteem the individual suffragette, and vice versa.

So in this vital matter of religion, we have the greatest consideration for the individual who may be in error, but for the error itself we have no tolerance. Christ Himself sets us the example in this by His love for the sinner, although He hated and denounced sin. In considering the various religions, we shall demonstrate that there is but one true religion, the others being consequently not true. But individuals in those others may be sincere, and if in the sight of God they are doing all in their power to live as God wants them to do, they are in a certain sense in the true Church, though not specifically so.

A man may be nominally a Socialist, yet his life and conduct might be altogether at variance with the logical platform of that party. So a person may be of a religious denomination which is false, and yet live superior to it. Cardinal Newman, who had the experience, said that a Protestant was, as a rule, better than his religion. I myself have received many persons from various denominations into the Catholic faith, and I have often found that at heart they were Catholics all along. By this I mean that, although Protestants, they were acting on Catholic principles, without knowing it. All the great saving truths of Protestantism are what were carried into it from the Catholic faith. There is not a single truth in Protestantism that does not exist in Catholicism. I say not a single *truth*, for you will find that everything that is absolutely true in every religion of the world is in the Catholic religion,—only without any admixture of error. But I am anticipating.

We have got to the point where we are to consider which is the true religion. From what I have said you will understand that we are considering the creed itself, not its adherents. We judge no man; that, we leave to God; but we can judge a creed, which is something tangible and subject to analysis. Now I am going to strike at the very heart of things at once, and show that there is but one religion in the world which is divine. In doing this, all the others necessarily must be rejected. You will understand that I am proceeding in all kindness and consideration.

To begin, then, I say that there is but one Church in the world that goes back directly to Jesus Christ. In establishing His religion, Christ said to Peter: "Upon thee I will build my church." This was a visible teaching church, with definite doctrine and external ritual. "Go ye forth into the whole world, teaching all things whatsoever I have commanded you, baptizing in the name of the Father and of the Son and of the Holy Ghost."

A teaching church is a visible church; a church which administers baptism is a church with an external ritual. Consequently we ask what church with a teaching ministry and external rites now exists in the world which goes back as a visible church to the very person of Peter and Jesus Christ. There is but one, the Catholic Church, whose head is the Pope, the successor of Peter and the representative of Christ. No other church dates its origin from the Apostolic times. Calvinists began with John Calvin in the sixteenth century, Lutherans began with Martin Luther, Episcopalians with Henry VIII, and so on.

But, you may say, the Protestant Church is the Church of Christ, purified of error, and only this purified form dates from Luther. I answer that you must choose between Luther and Christ. Jesus said His Church would never teach error; Luther says it did teach error. If Luther is right, Christ is wrong; but if Christ is right, Luther and all his followers are wrong.

But, you may say, was not the Church in a deplorable condition in the sixteenth century, were not the lives of some of its high clergy scandalous? I reply: yes, it is only too true, but Christ did not guarantee His Church against scandal, but against error. There were scandals in the Church even while Jesus was with it. Judas was a thief and a traitor and a suicide; Peter, the head, swore to a falsehood; James and John quarrelled over supremacy; St. Peter and St. Paul were at variance over circumcision; and Paul excommunicated one of the faithful for unspeakable lust.

The Church is made up of men not angels. The triumph of the Church is not in being composed of sinless mortals, but in supplying sinful man with means to carry on the struggle against his vicious tendencies. For that reason the Catholic Church has always been the friend of sinners, although hating sin. But Jesus by His divine power guaranteed that His Church, even if composed of weak and sinful men, would never teach error.

The Church may have needed housecleaning in the sixteenth century, but the way to clean house is not to dynamite it. A child may have a very dirty face, and yet be absolutely pure and healthy of skin. A doctor maybe a bad man but a very good doctor. And the Church may have been scandalous in the lives of some of its high dignitaries in the sixteenth century, but nevertheless it was absolutely free from error. A mother may be leading a very sinful life and yet guard her daughter from the same way of living and even teach her noble ideals.

I know personally of an unfortunate woman who, though steeped in vice herself, taught her daughter the highest morality. Afterwards the daughter became a nun, and when her mother was dying, an outcast in a city hospital, it was her daughter who held her dying head and helped her to call on God for the pardon He never refuses to the humble and contrite of heart. Should a daughter reform her mother by taking her life?

If God in His Providence and in order to show the inherent vitality of His Church permitted it to lapse in conduct, He did not allow it to err in doctrine. Indeed, He foresaw and foretold this very condition when He said: "The Scribes and Pharisees have sitten on the chair of Moses; do as they teach you but do ye not as they do."

The divinity of the Catholic Church shines out by the very fact that no matter what she may have been during the ages, her doctrine has always been true. Show me one false teaching of the Church in faith or morals during the past two thousand years, and I will grant you that she is not the Church of Christ.

Hurter, a very learned Protestant divine, who eventually became a Catholic and a champion of Catholicism, said that in dealing with Protestants and unbelievers it was a waste of time to go into historic details. History is often an uncertain witness, as we know. The writer's views are colored by his own bias. Take the great world war that began in 1914. If you read one side, you will think the other absolutely culpable, and *vice versa*. A world war has been going on for centuries in the realm of religion. The Church of Christ and the world have been and always will be at variance. Their spirit is essentially different. The world stands for time and material welfare, the Church stands for eternity and the welfare of the immortal soul. Hence the antagonism.

Consequently history reflects this antagonism. Facts in the life of the Catholic Church which constitute her greatest glory have been distorted into accusations against her. All down through the centuries she has stood for justice and has been the friend of the oppressed. No wonder if some of the mighty ones of earth who wished to have a free hand and who were restrained by her should calumniate her. And, as they were in power, they had the means of spreading their calumnies.

In sifting history, the task is interminable to pass on each individual case that comes up in the career of the Church. But this we know,—that history has proclaimed the death of the Church a hundred times. Generation after generation have mustered her out of service, but to-day she is the most widespread and united and vigorous organization in the world. Time and again she has seen the grass grow over the graves of those who have tolled her death knell. Nothing tests truth like time.

The best way to proceed with a Protestant inquirer is to get right down to incontrovertible ground. Was Jesus Christ God? Yes, or no? If no, there is no use proceeding, as the whole Christian platform falls and all, Christianity is an imposition. If He was God, He is divine Truth, and all that He says and promises is true. Did He establish a visible church? Yes, or no? If He did not, there is no use looking for it; if He did, then it is somewhere in the world to-day, for He declared it was to last until the end of the world.

Did He guarantee His Church against error? Yes, or no? If not, we never know when it must be believed; it is not a true guide; it cannot represent Him. If He did guarantee it against error, then it never has erred, for God's guarantee is indeed a guarantee. How, then, about the reformers? They were wrong,—either they, or Christ. But how about the state of the Church at various periods? Shocking, absolutely shocking. No one observed it more or lamented it more than the children of the Church. They were at times ashamed almost of their Mother; they labored and prayed for her betterment. Some of the greatest saints devoted their lives to remedying matters. But they never thought of denying their Mother.

If God saw fit to allow His Spouse to be at times weak and pitiable, it was to try the faith of His children and to show the vitality of their Mother. If the Church always stood forth plainly divine, there would be no astonishment at our faith in her, but to see in her the Spouse of Christ at all times because He declared that she was, that indeed is faith.

And she has justified it. If she were not divine, she would have perished a hundred times. But look at her now, the admiration of the world for her lofty teaching, her uncompromising dogma, her marvellous organization, her power over various peoples, her austere, divine principles! She has indeed seen fighting, she has been through many battles, at times she was hard fought, but has she not come through it all worthy of her Spouse, our divine Lord and Saviour, Jesus Christ?

Jesus Christ is God, He established one true Church, that Church is the Catholic Church.

CHAPTER XI.

How So Many are in Error

THE sight of so many prominent people who are not of the Catholic faith naturally makes us wonder if they are wrong and we right. In the United States what we call Society is for the most part Protestant. Society and wealth usually go together. In Belgium and France and Spain and Austria and other countries, society is mainly Catholic. I think I shall be able to show you most satisfactorily how so many of our eminent people are without the fold.

In the beginning of the sixteenth century, all Europe was Catholic. Then came a division called the Reformation. Martin Luther accused the Church of teaching error. As we have seen, Christ said His Church should never teach error. The Catholic Church at that time was the acknowledged Church of Christ, so it was a question between Christ and Luther. If the Church was in error, so was Christ, who had guaranteed it against error. Between Luther and Christ, we must stand with Christ and the Catholic Church.

But now see what happened. The Reformers claimed that they were separating from the Catholic Church because of its doctrine and morals. We should expect then that the Reformers would be men of high morality, and that their teaching would be the truth. What do we find? The leaders of the Reformation soon split up into numerous sects, each condemning the other, denying to others the right of interpretation they claimed for themselves, and soon created religious chaos. Their own morals and those of their followers were worse than those of the Church which they sought to reform. This is history.

Luther himself, after seeing the prevalent vice which his movement caused, exclaimed that the floodgates of sin and depravity were opened upon the people. Again, he declared that he would like to destroy with one stroke the great multitudes whom his own teaching had turned into a vicious horde. The morals were bad, the teaching was worse.

Truth is one and the same always. That is why the Catholic Church never changes. But each Reformer taught the contradictory of the other. If one was right, the others were wrong; that is as clear as day. You had Lutherans and

Calvinists, Baptists and Anabaptists, Episcopalians and Presbyterians, all contending among themselves, each declaring the other in error. And it was no minor error they accused each other of, but of vital and essential error; so much so that they fought and bled for their contention.

But what has all this got to do with the question we began with, namely, how is it that so many learned and respectable people are not Catholics if the Catholic Church is the true Church? What we have been touching on has everything to do with the matter, as you shall see. First of all, if these leaders are in error, their followers are also. But if they were in error, how did they get such a following? This is the very point of the whole question. I shall state the reason in brief form.

Certainly at first sight it seems impossible that so many people as the Protestant sects number should be misled, that they should be in error. Well, now, just see how it happened. As in the world war there are millions of men engaged on both sides who hold that they are right, and yet both sides are not right, so in the upheaval of the sixteenth century.

In the Reformation, the leaders had personal motives for their stand. They appealed to the pride and independence and passion and covetousness of human nature. To those in power they pointed out the wealth to be gained by confiscating Church property, and the independence they would have by separating from the Mother Church and its authority. With some temporal princes thus won over, and by making the new religion easy for the people at large, the reformers gradually won over a considerable following.

It would take me too far out of the way to go into details in this regard and to give the proofs of all that I state. I am giving the mere outlines. Consult the history of the period, and you will find substantiation for all I advance. But do not take Protestant authors only.

In passing I will merely say that in England Henry VIII either put to death or put into prison everyone of importance who did not follow him in his revolt from the Mother Church. What was the result? In the beginning, some joined the Protestant movement for gain, some for license, and some to escape imprisonment and death. The princes in their endeavor to justify their position did all in their power to blacken the Church that they had separated from.

In consequence, as in England, no one was allowed to speak or write in defence of the Catholic Church. On the other hand, the land was filled with literature abusing and misrepresenting Catholicity. After years of persecution and calumny, the people at large hardly knew the truth. Gradually the new generations took it for granted that the religion they were born in and which they saw by law established was the true one, and they simply continued in it.

The very sources of truth were poisoned, so that later those who investigated the claims of their religion came back to these false documents.

Newman, who was one of the most learned Protestants of the past three centuries, declares that English history since the sixteenth century has been a conspiracy against truth. Now he was virtually the pope of Protestantism and his words should carry conviction. Newman, a born Protestant, a learned Protestant, a good Protestant, a man who believed that Rome was Babylon and the Pope Antichrist, this man opposed to the Roman Catholic Church and to everything about it simply because it was born in him; this man of gigantic intellect, eventually saw, in spite of his environment of prejudice, that the Catholic Church was the one true Church of Christ.

The reason so many people are not Catholics is because so many have been robbed of their inheritance of truth. They go on in the religion they find themselves in, hardly giving it a thought, taking it for granted that it is the true religion. But when they do go seriously at analyzing their position, they find that it has no foundation, and they give up religious faith altogether or become Catholics. That is the experience of thousands, hundreds of thousands. The best and most intellectual of Protestants are the ones who, if they investigate, become Catholics.

Recently Protestantism has been going from bad to worse. It has been broken up into innumerable sects, so that now it has no fixed creed. Truth never changes. Protestantism is disintegrating into rationalism, infidelity, materialism. Most of the inquirers who come to me for information on religion tell me that they are Protestants in name only. They do not know what they should believe; in fact, they have no definite creed.

Contrast that with the Catholic Church. It has not changed one article of faith from the day of the Apostles to our own. That does not mean that it is a fossil. It is the most active organization in the world to-day. The multiplication table has not changed in the past two thousand years. It is not a fossil. The truth never changes.

My answer, then, to the question of why so many who are of other sects can be in error is this: They take it for granted that the religion they are born in is true. Their ancestors were robbed of the true faith by violence, flattery, and worldy inducements. History and literature have been perverted to serve the cause of error. But those who sincerely investigate usually come back to the Mother Church, the Church founded by Christ, the Catholic Church.

Lest it may seem that the foregoing statements represent an unfriendly or extreme view of the matter, I quote the following from *the Athenæum* (London).

"There is no living writer more thoroughly equipped for producing a trustworthy work on the English Reformation than Dr. Gairdner (non-Catholic). Now that the one man in all England who has the whole of the facts at his fingers' ends has spoken with such deliberation, no decent writer, however stanchly antipapist in his convictions, ought to cite Legh or Layton to substantiate tales of the vicious lives of the monks. 'It was only after an able and despotic King,' says Gairdner, 'had proved himself stronger than the spiritual power of Rome that the people of England were divorced from the Roman allegiance; and there is abundant evidence that they were divorced from it against their will.'"

These statements and others of a similar nature touching on the Bible, the Pope, and the general religious condition of the times evoke the following comment from the *Sacred Heart Review*. "The chief points of attack on the Catholic Church in England have been abandoned under the leadership of one of our sanest Protestant scholars. At any rate no 'decent writer' in the words of the *Athenæum*, will now repeat the slanders against the monks, or claim that the Bible was given to England by Wycliffe or Tyndale, or deny that the Pope fostered civil and religious liberty, or that he was revered by England as the Vicar of Christ."

CHAPTER XII.

How So Many are Indifferent

IT may be asked why, if religion is divine and so important to man, some are indifferent to it. We have seen that God has done His part. But religion is a bond between God and man. It requires man's efforts as well as God's goodness. God has been good enough to come on earth and establish His Church for all. He invites, pleads, commands all to enter. But He allows every man liberty. God forces no one to serve Him. If men choose to be indifferent to His commands, which are for their own good, He, because He has created them free, will leave them to their own wilfulness.

But where one's everlasting welfare is concerned, why should anyone be indifferent? I may ask why are so many people indifferent to their health, which is essential for real living. The drunkard, the libertine, the drug fiend, all perceive that they are ruining their health, yet they keep on. And why? Because they satisfy themselves in one way or another for the time being.

So those who are indifferent to religion are so because they have regard only to what concerns their present indulgence. Anything that does not promise gain or pleasure they care not for. But you say that such an attitude is unreasonable. So it is. Scripture says: "The fool hath said in his heart, there is no God." It is only the fool who so acts. And no matter what ability or success a man has, if he be without concern for his soul, for religion, for eternity, he is a fool. God says: "What doth it profit a man if he gain the whole world and lose his soul?" In the face of that divine declaration we should pity those who are indifferent, and pray for them.

There are, unfortunately, men and women who give more thought to the next season's styles than they do to the next world. But, without doing violence to their free will, God can do no more to bring them to the right way.

But the day of realization will come at last, the day when every human being must stand before God and give an account of his stewardship. This life is only a step, and a short one, in our existence. It brings us to the true life of eternity. How careful we should be to take that step rightly!

CHAPTER XIII.

RATIONALISM AND MATERIALISM

IN the world to-day there are two specious classes of men who are opposed to Jesus Christ and to Christianity. I call them specious because they appear under the banner of enlightenment. They take their stand as thinkers and scientists, and in this form they make a strong appeal to persons who respect reason above all other endowments. Reason is our most valued endowment, and we should hold it in the highest consideration. Jesus Christ Himself so regarded it.

No scientist or philosopher in all history regarded reason as highly as Christ. No philosopher made such a strong appeal to it as did He. He told the Jews plainly to reject Him and His doctrine if He did not give them the best of reasons for their believing in Him. Do not believe me, He said, because I say a thing, but because I substantiate it. If you do not believe me, at least believe the works which I do. You can see and verify them. They speak for me.

You see, He gave an actual demonstration of His proposition as a mathematician does in a class-room. It is as if a man were to tell a native of South Africa that ether waves existed and could be controlled by human contrivances so as to send a message around the world. If the hearer denied or doubted, the speaker would forthwith send a message and demonstrate the truth of his statement.

So Jesus Christ did. When the Jews doubted His divinity and His mission, He said to them: I declare myself the true Son of God, the Messias. You hesitate to believe me. Indeed I know how wonderful my claims are, I realize your difficulty, I know how you regard the Almighty, and for this reason I am prepared to meet your difficulties. To demonstrate my statements, I consequently manifest the power which only God can exercise. Believe my works, *they give testimony of me*. Before your eyes you see men who were born blind now seeing as well as yourselves, you behold the leper cleansed, the cripple made whole, yea, there walk among you men who were dead and whom you were carrying out to burial and whom I by a word called back to life. *These my works give testimony of me.*

Is there any scientist or philosopher in the world who could show greater respect for reason than Jesus Christ! But once He gives His credentials, He speaks with authority. To listen to and believe one who is divine is not the surrendering of reason, but its most noble exercise.

See how learned men listen to Edison and Marconi and accept wonderful things from them merely on their word for it. Do people consider that as unreasonable? Not at all. Yet a greater one than Edison, a millionfold greater, speaks, and rationalists say that it is unreasonable to believe Him. Scientists do not regulate our morals, Christ does; that is the difference.

In our chapters on the spirituality and immortality of the soul, we showed how untenable is the position of materialists. We shall now proceed to demonstrate that the rationalists, the worshippers of human reason, form but a specious cult, their mind and reason being swayed not by evidence, but by passion, in one form or another. Their principle is to submit everything to reason, and to reject whatever they do not understand. As they are unable to comprehend some of the teachings of Jesus Christ, they refuse to accept His religion.

It is true that, as rational beings, we should submit things to investigation and refuse to admit them if they are against reason. God gave us our intellects for that very purpose. But the doctrine of Jesus Christ, which is undoubtedly above our comprehension, above our reason, is not opposed to reason. We do not accept it because we understand it, but because we know that He who declares it cannot proclaim anything but the truth.

The most intelligent people act in a like manner every day. After they make sure by reasonable inquiry that a person is competent and trustworthy, they accept from him many things that they do not understand. It is thus we act with physicians, chemists, electricians, engineers, etc. But, you will say, if we do not understand, we know that those we trust understand, and we could, also, if we applied our minds to the matter. Very true. What I wish to emphasize is that in point of fact we take many vital things on the word of another in whom we trust, simply because of our confidence in his integrity and knowledge.

Now I ask you if Jesus Christ, who is divine truth, is not worthy of our trust? Can we doubt His integrity or knowledge? Is it not, then, the highest use of our reason to conclude that He who gave it to us can be trusted absolutely?

Reason all you wish about the divinity of Christ, but once that is admitted it is most reasonable to believe every word He utters. If He, out of His goodness or to give us the opportunity of exercising faith in Him, reveals things to us that our reason never could excogitate, it is our loving duty to accept the revelation. If what He reveals mystifies us, it is only what we should expect when we contemplate divinity.

See how many natural things mystify us. Who can understand the law of gravitation? Who knows the nature of electricity? An ordinary student knows how to produce electricity and can utilize it, but all the scientists together cannot tell us what electricity is. The greatest minds among them have exercised their ingenuity for years, but all they can do is to theorize; they have nothing certain to tell us of its nature.

And if we cannot understand nature, should we be amazed that we do not understand nature's God? Do rationalists reject gravitation and electricity, etc., because they cannot understand their nature? Why, then, should they reject the religion of Jesus Christ because they cannot understand its sublime truths? If the religion of Christ did not require man to shape his life by it, no one would reject it.

Take the matter of Jesus Christ, for example. Those opposed to the Christian religion, if they are logical and consistent, are obliged to admit that if He is God what He says is true. How, then, do they avoid it? They either deny that He is God, or affirm that He did not mean just what He said. In carrying out their purpose, they act differently in His case from what they do in any other. In any court of law, if a man's character is proved upright and his mind is sound, he is believed. All the world agrees that Christ's character is the most perfect in the history of the human race, and that His mind is the loftiest and sanest of which we have record. Why, then, is He not accorded the same rational acceptance that is given others?

They call themselves rationalists, when in the very exercise of reason they act unreasonably. Yet they regard with pity the poor believers! There would be no rationalism if Christ did not demand along with belief also practice.

In conclusion, I should like a rationalist to consider the following points. It is historically certain that Jesus Christ changed the face of the earth. He found the great Roman Empire pagan; He made it Christian. This was accomplished by means which were, humanly considered, absolutely inadequate. Christ was poor, His apostles were poor, His followers were poor. He had no army, no influential associates, no prestige, no human inducements. On the other hand, His religion was opposed to all that flatters human nature. It inculcated the loftiest virtue, the sternest morality, and demanded the greatest self-sacrifice. For three hundred years imprisonment, exile, and death threatened the recruit to Christianity, yet it spread rapidly over the then known world.

How such a religion ever got a foothold in the world is as great a mystery as the Trinity. If you are looking for miracles, there is one. Well could St. Augustine exclaim: "The establishment of the Catholic Church without miracles is a greater miracle than any recorded in Scripture. But if in its establishment there were miracles, you must acknowledge its divinity." Hence, with or without miracles, the Catholic Church stands forth a divine creation.

The Catholic Church, then, is divine. Is it any wonder that Catholics love it and live for it and, if need be, die for it? We know what we have; we do not merely opine. And realizing that our Church is divine, we listen to her as to Christ. If in the course of her history she has had human failings, we know that although she is divine, she is also human, and that Christ prepared us for scandals. But, above all, we know that, weak though she may be in her human element, she is supported by God Himself and guaranteed by Him to be a messenger of Truth always.

Her frailties make her sympathize with her children, and also give God an opportunity of showing that by the weak things of this world He confounds the strong. The weaker she is in herself, the more divine she proves herself to be. For during twenty centuries, all the power of the world has been employed against her only to leave her stronger after each struggle. All the passions of corrupt human nature have risen up against her, only to find her ever championing virtue and triumphing over evil.

This spectacle in the world is indeed a miracle. It is religion's reply to the challenge of unbelief. It is reason's answer to rationalists.

CHAPTER XIV.

ACCUSATIONS AGAINST THE TRUE CHURCH

THERE are many sincere people who really believe that the Catholic Church has a record which disqualifies her as the true Church. They point out instances in history which seem incompatible with an organization that represents Christ. This is worth looking into.

First of all, I wish to say that if the Catholic Church were what she is represented to be by her opponents, we Catholics would be as eager as they to destroy her. If the Catholic Church is a hundredth part as bad as she is pictured by her enemies, she cannot be the Church of Christ.

I am far from holding that there were no abuses in the Church. But they were the abuses which more or less had been attached to her from the beginning, and which Christ foretold.

Christ guaranteed His Church against error, not against scandal. His own little Church of twelve had abuses, for Peter denied Him and Judas was a thief and a suicide. But apart from the abuses of human weakness, which have always characterized the Church, her Reformation enemies accused her of crimes and teachings which were absolutely without foundation.

Well, what about history, you say, can we not trust history, and does not history point out manifold abuses and evils in the Church of Rome? To this let me say that many a scholar who consulted history in order to substantiate charges against the Catholic Church has ended by becoming a Catholic himself. Can we not trust history? Yes, history that is really history, but you cannot trust the history of an adversary. Suppose in this great world war which is now waging you read only what one side has to say, what would you think about the other? There are millions of people who have never got a bit of information about the Catholic Church except from hostile sources.

History is now being rewritten. Scholars who go deeply into the matter are unanimous in their verdict that the Catholic Church has been consistently maligned during the past four centuries. This is so evident that a number of distinguished writers have declared that history has been distorted in order to uphold the sects opposed to the Catholic Church. I cite in proof of this statement one notable name, Dr. James Gairdner, the foremost authority today in matters pertaining to the Reformation period in England.

Dr. Gairdner, who is not a Catholic, had access to all the state papers and documents bearing on the Reformation and afterwards, and he shows conclusively that the facts were altogether misrepresented and even falsified. Here is a man who had unusual opportunities for research: he was not a Catholic, he was under the prevailing English prejudice against the Catholic Church, yet the results of his scientific investigations make it evident that history was perverted to defame the Church of Rome and to aid the cause of the Reformation.

John Henry Newman says the same thing. His testimony should count, for he was a Protestant of Protestants. For years he opposed the Church of Rome. In studying history to get facts to justify his position, his eyes were opened. He saw a great light and had the courage to follow it, even though it led him into the Church he opposed, and of which he afterwards became the great champion.

Can you imagine that a man of Newman's lofty intellect and pure life would embrace the Catholic Faith if it were what people outside that Faith declare it to be! In the chapter entitled "How so many are in error," you will find further data bearing on this point.

But were there no abuses in the history of the Church? Many, very many, enough to wreck her if she were not divine. Christ foretold that there would be scandals in the Church and warned His followers against them. Our Lord did not guarantee His Church against evil members, but against false doctrine. He plainly states that the wheat and cockle will grow together until the harvest. He established His Church for sinners. That is what the sacraments are for,—to reclaim the sinner and to sanctify the just. His mission on earth was among sinners,—witness Magdalene, the woman of Samaria, the penitent thief. Even among the chosen twelve there was a thief and traitor.

The Church of Christ is for the sinner as well as the saint. In the course of ages, she met the Goth and the Hun and the Vandal and moulded them into Christians. In this process she had strenuous labor. It is not to be wondered at if, in this work of transformation, many things happened which shock our modern sensibilities.

But you may say that you understand very well that among the flock there should be some black sheep, but how about the shepherds? Were not the very men who constituted the government of the Church frequently bad? To this I say that in the history of the world there is no body of men that can at all compare with the pastors of the Church for virtue and learning. Having said this, I now add that it is only too true that here and there at certain periods there were shepherds unworthy of the name. Even this Christ foretold when He said: "The Scribes and Pharisees have sitten upon the chair of Moses; all things whatsoever they shall say to you, observe and do, but according to their works, do ye not."

It is as hard for a clergyman to be good as for a layman. Both are made of the same clay. Christ never said that those in authority would be saints. Thank God, for the most part they are good men, but not because they are in high places, but because they make good use of the graces given them. But if they neglect, they will fall just as an ordinary person. This does not affect the Church, however, but only themselves. In a certain way it affects the Church, by reason of the bad example they give, but no Catholic thinks any the less of his Church because one of its ministers is recreant.

God can and does use even a bad man to do His work. David was guilty of murder and adultery. Solomon fell into idolatry and lust. Yet both were the anointed leaders of God's people.

The United States appoints judges to represent her in the various federal districts. An individual may be a very bad man, yet a good judge, whose decisions are always respected. So in the Church, those in authority may occasionally slip, some may be utterly unworthy of their place, yet, as ministers of religion, they have God's power back of them. Above all there is one who, no matter what he be, has the guarantee of Christ that he will never teach false doctrine as head of the Church and that is Peter and his successors, the popes.

It is as hard for a Catholic to be good as it is for anyone else. We are all human. There is a great difference between knowing what is right and doing it. St. Paul exclaimed that while he was preaching to others he feared he himself might become a castaway. When Christ Himself was on earth, He had frequently to upbraid His followers for their delinquencies. He even said on one occasion: "Have I not chosen you," speaking to His apostles, "yet one of you is a devil."

It is related of St. Augustine that one of his monks, having left the monastery and gone to the neighboring city, gave great scandal there. The people were infuriated and went in a body to destroy the monastery. Augustine met them and said: "You are astonished that one of my monks has betrayed his calling and given scandal. Why should you be amazed and incensed because one out of my three hundred has gone wrong when one out of our Lord's twelve was bad?" This remark brought them to their senses, and they returned to the city forthwith.

The Catholic Church is made up of human beings and they are not forced to be good. What is right is always held up to them and they have every encouragement to do it, but they are free. It is safe to say that if all Catholics lived up to their religion, the world could not hold out against conversion. But it is not easy to be a good Catholic. It calls for the restraint of passion and the exercise of virtue. Individual Catholics under strong temptation have fallen.

Lust, ambition, power, wealth, have led many astray. But they all knew they were doing wrong, they knew they were going against the Church's teaching, they never attempted to justify wrongdoing. There have been, even among high churchmen, men of evil lives, but the Church never condoned them. The Catholic Church never connived at sin. It never allowed that wrong was right. Always it stood forth protesting when it could not prevent evil.

In England the Church could have continued in full authority if she had been willing to compromise on the sacredness of marriage. But, like John the Baptist, she said to Henry VIII: "It is not lawful." It is well to weigh this fact, that those who set out to reform the Church of Rome introduced divorce into Christianity. While the Catholic Church lost the realm of England for upholding God's law of marriage, the reformers in Germany granted a violation of that law to gain over to their forces a small principality. This is a fact that talks more than pages and volumes of statement.

History may be distorted, but facts are stubborn things, and this one is an indication that the Catholic Church is the voice of Christ in the world. No merely human organization would stem so powerful a current as the lust and power of Henry VIII forced against the Catholic Church. She never winked at sin. Always her voice rang out in protest no matter who the culprit might be.

Until the sixteenth century, there was no such thing among Christians as divorce. To-day, the Catholic Church alone stands out against it. Before the sixteenth century, there was no race suicide among Christians. To-day, the Catholic Church alone stands uncompromisingly against it. Now these things are indications. They are before our eyes. We can see them for ourselves. They furnish a key to history.

If the Church to-day, in spite of the evil lives of some of her members, stands out like Christ saying "Thou shalt not," does it not show us her character? If to-day she stands for what is right in what concerns the dominant passion of mankind, is it not an index of her sanctity throughout the ages?

If this were a longer treatise, I could take up various matters, one by one, and show how, from the beginning, the Catholic Church held up the highest standards. When, therefore, we meet with things in history which seem incompatible with a divine Church, how are we to regard them? In every instance they are the result not of the teaching of the Church, but of the violation of her teaching. They show the passion and weakness of individuals, not the doctrine of the Church.

Benedict Arnold's treason does not mean that American generals were mercenary. It is no reflection on American patriotism. Neither does the evil life of a distinguished churchman signify that the Church is corrupt. In some of our cities, at times, a corrupt ring gets control, but that does not mean that government by the people must be abolished.

But why, you may say, was not the Church, if divine, able to prevent her adherents from evil deeds. The wonder is that she prevented as much as she did. To-day the Catholic Church is the only organization on earth that prevents divorce. She alone takes a stand against and stops race suicide. In our own country, where the Sunday service is fast disappearing, she alone makes it obligatory on her members to worship God on Sunday by attendance at public service. Do not these facts speak for themselves? Do they not give you a clue in reading history, and should they not make you suspicious of the charges made against her?

As a present-day instance, to confirm what I have been stating, let us consider an oft-repeated charge against the Church. There is a cry periodically raised in certain quarters that loyalty to Rome means disloyalty to one's own country. If you read history, so-called, you will find charges made against

Catholics that they are not and cannot be patriotic. Now I shall name one instance which is at present before us all and which knocks to pieces this and similar accusations.

What nation to-day in all the world is hailed as the most patriotic? Belgium. What individual stands out as the most patriotic figure in this great World War? Cardinal Mercier. Belgium is a Catholic country. Cardinal Mercier is a Catholic prelate. To a man who reflects, this is conclusive.

A Catholic would be just as desirous of doing away with his Church as her opponents are if she were not divine. We have examined every line of history, and if there were one instance in which the Church upheld wrong, we would renounce her. What do we get by being loyal to her? Nothing, here below. But when we know that Christ established a Church and guaranteed it against false teaching, we realize that she is the safe guide to eternal life.

In being faithful to her, we know that we are doing what God wants us to do. And if He wants us to do a thing, it does not matter what our likes or dislikes may be, our duty is plain. Having God's guarantee that His Church is our sure guide to a blessed immortality, that she is the pillar and ground of truth, we read history in the light of that guarantee. Unless that guarantee holds, all Christianity falls; it is an imposition. But God's word holds.

CHAPTER XV.

ATTITUDE OF THE TRUE BELIEVER

THE inquirer into religion is urged to use all the reason God has given him to make sure that Christ is God and that He has established a divine Church. Also he is encouraged to use his reason to make certain that the Catholic Church is the one Church established by Christ. Once having settled that, it is in perfect accord with reason to accept without questioning all that this divine Church teaches.

It is no slavery of intellect to bow down before divine truth. In traversing an unknown and dangerous country, a man shows wisdom in submitting to an accredited guide. Suppose someone should deride him for trusting in his guide. He would reply that such trust showed common sense.

So God has given us His Church to guide us safely by the pitfalls of life, and in trusting her we show, not feebleness, but intelligence. Our attitude to the Church should therefore be like that of St. Paul, who exclaimed when Christ appeared to him on the way to Damascus: "Lord, what wilt thou have me to do?" We should go to the Church as a child to its mother, with perfect trust and love. If she tells us what principles are to guide us in life, we should receive them as from God. If she points out the way that leads to eternal life, we should follow it. If she tells us that certain things are dangerous, we should hearken to her. If she gives us help to strengthen us in our soul's warfare, we should welcome them.

In a word, we should hear her words and follow her guidance as we would those of God Himself. In doing this we are merely carrying out Christ's injunction, for He said of His Church: "He who hears you, hears me." If our Lord's words mean anything, they mean just that. That is why St. Paul called the clergy the ambassadors of Christ. When they declare the authoritative teaching of the Church, they announce the truth of God.

This constitutes the great comfort and security of Catholics. They know; they do not conjecture. They have certitude, not probability. They are not searching for the light; they have it. That is why Catholics are so firm, so uncompromising. Truth has nothing to compromise. We do not compromise on the multiplication table. The truths of the Catholic Church are just as certain, for the Church is God speaking to His people.

If on reading thus far you are convinced of the truth of the Catholic Church, it remains for you to accept her doctrine and to live by it. I shall accordingly put before you briefly the leading points of the true religion.

If you are not convinced of the truth of the Catholic Church, I request you to pray. Jesus Christ, the Living Truth and the Light of the World, was rejected by some of His own people. It was not because He was not the Truth or Light, but because, as St. John says, the Light shone in the darkness and the darkness did not comprehend it. The failure to comprehend was not the fault of the Light.

Therefore, pray. Pray for light to know the truth and strength to follow it. For many are afraid to know the truth for fear of it. It might cause a change in the manner of their life or in their prospects. So courage is needed as well as light. If you do your part, God will do His.

In the second part, which follows, there is a brief exposition of Catholic teaching and an inquiry into the different dogmas. It will be found serviceable for prospective converts, and, it is hoped, will help a busy priest in his work of instruction, for it explains nearly all the things which usually present difficulties to inquirers.

It strikes me that the point of view which makes people formulate their own religion and which constitutes it auto-religion is the dominant feature of the present attitude outside the Church. In consequence they view the Church as narrow, unprogressive and even fossilized. The mariner's compass might be condemned on their view because it always points the same, yet it is this fixedness which gives it its value. Any variation in the established nature of the compass would not be progress but ruin. A navigator is not considered narrow because he holds to the compass, neither is a Catholic narrow who holds to the Church. The compass is nature's provision for guiding the mariner over the trackless water, the Church is the provision of nature's God for the guidance of men over the sea of life.

The Church loves nothing so much as light. The brighter the light and the more it penetrates her every feature the more she stands forth the true bride of Christ. Christ not only loved the light but was the very light itself. "I the light am come into the world that whosoever believeth in Me may not remain in darkness." And Isaias seeing the Church in vision exclaims, "Thou shalt no more have the sun for thy light, but the Lord shall be unto thee for an everlasting light and thy God for thy glory." Jesus Christ and His Church! The divine Bridegroom and His Bride! Our Father who art in Heaven—and on earth Our Holy Mother the Church!

PART II.

THE PRINCIPAL TEACHING OF THE CATHOLIC CHURCH

CHAPTER I.

WHY THERE ARE MYSTERIES IN RELIGION

PEOPLE often wonder what is the use of religious truths that we cannot understand. What purpose does a mystery serve in our relations with God? Why should there be matters in our Faith which are above our comprehension?

On a little thought the reason for mysteries will be plain.

First of all, they enable us to make an act of faith in God. If God gave us truths which we could reason out for ourselves, we should not be trusting to His truthfulness but to our intelligence. If you take from God only what you can verify, you are treating Him as you do your fellow-man. Indeed, hardly as well, for you take many things from your fellow-man which you do not and cannot verify. It is only one man in a million who understands matters of history, science, and government, yet all have faith in these things. See how we trust our lives and national honor to the ruler of our country.

He frequently does not and cannot give an explanation of his policy. Facts which he has and which justify his actions must be kept secret for reasons of the public welfare. Yet we have such confidence in his intelligence and integrity that we trust him. That is our act of faith in the government, in a man. Should we not trust to the integrity and intelligence of the Ruler of the world?

If, therefore, God sees fit to tell us something which we could never know by our own reason, why not accept it as an acquisition to our knowledge and be grateful for it? How many things the astronomer and chemist and historian tell us which most of us cannot reason out and yet which we accept gladly. All life may be said to be an act of faith in one another. Why, then, should we not make an act of faith in God?

Now if there were no mysteries, we could not make an act of faith in God. A mystery is something above reason, but not against it. It is something which, though not implying a contradiction, is yet so full of difficulty that we have to exclaim: How can it be! God simply says: "It is so, trust me."

There are mysteries in our own lives, mysteries in the world about us. If you told anyone before Columbus' time that there were people on the other side of the world, they would say: "Impossible! How can it be! They would fall off, they would be head downwards!" If the law of gravitation solves the difficulty, why may not God, in His own time, solve all the mysteries? One of the joys of heaven will be that we shall understand everything.

I cannot say it too often,—God does not want us to understand Him, but to trust Him. If He sees fit to reveal to us certain things about Himself which we could never of ourselves learn, why not thank Him? Should we not expect God to be a mysterious Being? Nature is mysterious, why should not nature's God be so?

If, then, there are revelations about the mysterious God, they must be in the nature of mysteries. A man is a mystery to himself. He does not know how his mind commands his body, nor how he remembers things, nor how things outside of him are by eating turned into his own body. If man is a mystery to man himself, why should not Almighty God be a mystery to him?

In imparting to us, therefore, information about Himself, as in the Trinity and Incarnation and the Eucharist, we should expect mysteries. It is for that reason that our religion is called our holy Faith. It is based on faith in God. Its foundation is the veracity of God. We know that God is Truth, that if He says something it is so, and accordingly we say: "Speak, Lord, thy servant heareth."

Through the Church God speaks to us. In the following chapters, we shall see what that message is. Our duty is to accept it gratefully, and, by doing as directed, to merit one day to see face to face the Infinite God in whose light we shall be enlightened and in whose presence we shall rejoice forevermore. "Eye hath not seen, nor ear heard, nor hath it entered into the mind of man to conceive the things that God hath prepared for them that love Him."

CHAPTER II.

The Trinity

THE Trinity is a wonderful mystery. No one understands it. The most learned theologian, the holiest Pope, the greatest saint, all are as mystified by it as the child of seven. It is one of the things which we shall know only when we see God face to face. If God saw fit to reveal His nature to us without explaining it, that is His condescension. Anything we may know about the marvellous Creator is a favor. Of course from the universe we gain a certain knowledge of Him. We know He is infinitely Wise and Powerful. But about His person we can know nothing of ourselves.

Now, in the mystery of the Trinity, He tells us something about His personality. He says it is three-fold. Mark, He does not say that there are three Gods in one God, nor three Persons in one Person. That would be a contradiction, and our reason tells us that contradictions are not true. God would not tell us something which the reason He gave us should be obliged to reject.

What, then, does He say in the revelation of the Trinity? He informs us that in the one Being, God, there are three Persons. He calls these three Persons the Father, Son, and Holy Ghost. Not till we get to heaven shall we know any more than that. If we reason from now to doomsday, we shall not get any nearer to an explanation, and simply because God said that much and no more.

Theologians have written thousands of volumes in analyzing and inquiring into the matter, but merely as speculation, just as we speculate about planetary motion and the number of the stars and the spots on the moon. Only there is some chance of learning something about these things, none of learning anything further about the Trinity.

Jesus Christ said: "The Father and I are one." One what? Not one person, surely, for two persons cannot be one person. A man can say Smith and I are one. One what? Perhaps one corporation, one team, one race, one pair. Of course it is not in the same sense that Christ spoke. I merely endeavor to show by comparison that there is no contradiction in the statement.

When Jesus sent His apostles forth to convert the world, He commanded them to baptize in the name of the Father and of the Son and of the Holy Ghost. Mark, He does not say in the names, but in the *name*,—one. At the baptism of Jesus, a voice from heaven proclaimed: "This is my beloved Son, hear ye Him." Christ on the cross said: "Father, forgive them, they know not what they do." Here is the relation of Father and Son, and each is God. Yet there is but one God. "Hearken, O Israel, the Lord thy God is one only. There is no other God beside me." (Deut. xxx. 39.)

That Jesus is the true Son of God, and, consequently, God like the Father, is evident from Scripture: "No man hath seen God at any time: the Only Begotten Son, who is in the bosom of the Father, hath declared Him." (John i. 18.) Jesus is proclaimed the Only Begotten Son of God. Therefore His is a true divine nature, He is true God. There is therefore something about the nature of God by which in one Godhead there can be more than one person. What that is we do not know. And God does not want us to know,—yet.

In the commission which Jesus gives to His apostles, He names three persons equally: Baptize in the *name* of the *Father* and of the *Son* and of the *Holy Ghost*. These three constitute the Blessed Trinity, to whom be honor and glory forever!

CHAPTER III.

The Incarnation

THE Incarnation and the Trinity are the fundamental mysteries of the Catholic Faith. On these two everything else rests. If there is no Trinity, then there is no redemption by the Second Person of the Trinity. If there is no Incarnation, there is no atonement by Jesus Christ, the God-man.

The word Incarnation is derived from the two Latin words *in* and *caro*, which mean *in the flesh*. As applied to the Son of God, they signify His existence in the flesh, that is, His becoming man. This is a stupendous mystery, as difficult of comprehension as the Trinity. How the infinite God became finite man, yet remained God, is something we do not understand. It was so difficult of apprehension for the Jews, who had a true conception of God, that they could not or would not believe that Christ was God. That was their whole contention. Because He affirmed He was God, they put Him to death.

Jesus realized their difficulty and met it sympathetically. He told them that no man was a witness to his own word, and referred them for proof of His word to His deeds: "The things which I do give testimony of me."

And those Jews who were not influenced by passion recognized His testimony. From the beginning of the world, said they, no man spoke as this man, and no man ever did the things which he does. Thus spoke the multitudes.

On one occasion, Jesus forgave a man his sins. "Who but God can forgive sins?" the Scribes and Pharisees exclaimed. Jesus accepted their challenge. True, said He, no one but God can forgive sins, but that you may know that I have the power to forgive sins, that I am indeed God, I shall do something before your eyes which only God can do. And straightway He said to the cripple, who was brought to Him on a bed: "Take up thy bed and walk." And the man arose and walked, and all glorified God. This is but one of hundreds of things which Jesus did to show the people that they could trust Him. Once He established His divine power, it was their duty to believe Him.

And the great body of people did believe in Him. But the Scribes and Pharisees, who saw that their sway over the multitude would cease with their acceptance of Jesus as the Messias, used all their power to discredit Him. A dreadful instance of this is in regard to their conduct after the resurrection of Lazarus.

I once said to a distinguished lawyer that, as an example of the bad faith of the Jewish leaders, their attempt to suppress evidence in the case of Lazarus was convincing proof. He asked me in just what way they tried to do so. I informed him that after the resurrection of Lazarus, which was witnessed by hundreds, among whom were many distinguished men of Jerusalem, the Jews called a council. In this council, they debated how they could kill Lazarus so as to destroy the proof of his resurrection. The lawyer exclaimed: "Why, I never saw that in Scripture. If that is so, it is conclusive, for in law the suppression of evidence is the most flagrant criminality." He then asked me to point out the passage in Scripture which recorded the fact. I did so, and he said no greater proof could exist of malicious intent against Christ. (John xii. 10.)

In this connection, let me say that the Jews themselves never denied the miracles of Jesus. The Scriptures, taken merely as profane history, record the doings of Christ as they occurred and as they were accepted by the people generally. Unless His deeds were just as recorded in the Bible, the Jews would have protested against the narration from the start. They never did.

It may be asked, why, then, did they not receive Jesus Christ as the Messiah? The reply is that He did not give them what they wanted. They expected a worldly kingdom and a mighty temporal ruler who would exalt their nation above all others. But Christ did not leave heaven and come to this earth to give the fleeting things of this world to man. He came to give eternal life, an eternal kingdom. Hence He said: "My kingdom is not of this world." The Scribes and Pharisees were looking merely to the present. Hence they rejected their greatest good, they renounced Jesus Christ. How many to-day reject Jesus because He does not give them what they want here!

CHAPTER IV.

The Redemption

THE Redemption, or the Atonement, as it is sometimes called, signifies the passion and death of Jesus Christ by which mankind was restored to the friendship and favor of God. The Redemption implies that man had offended God, and in consequence lost something. In theology this is called the fall of man.

It may be humiliating for us to acknowledge it, but it must nevertheless be admitted that there is something wrong with human nature. Man is a bundle of contradictions, a combination of heaven and earth. He admires what is noble, yet constantly tends to what is degrading. He is master of the rest of creation, yet frequently a slave to his own passions. He is a strange mixture of greatness and littleness, of good and evil. A man is often astonished at his own meanness, while astonishing others by his magnanimity. Often he finds himself doing the things he hates and detests, again omitting what he most approves of.

The world seems to be out of joint,—everywhere misunderstandings, rivalries, jealousies, selfishness, quarrels. There seem to be two personalities warring within us. Stevenson has characterized this in his Dr. Jekyll and Mr. Hyde. I am sure we have often seen, either in ourselves or others, the counterpart of that description.

Is it possible that man so constituted is the work of God? Rather, does he not proclaim that he is a masterpiece marred?

The religion of Jesus Christ gives the solution of this enigma when it tells us that man is fallen from his high estate. Let those who ridicule the doctrine of original sin find a substitute for the cause of man's deplorable condition. The Church teaches us that by the wilful transgression of our first parents our nature as endowed in them became impaired. And, as a man forfeiting an inheritance by his conduct also deprives his descendants of it, so the loss of God's favor by our first parents entailed a loss on their descendants. That loss of God's grace is original sin.

Man's destiny was to live on for a certain time and, after proving his loyalty to God, to enter heaven as his home. God could have pardoned sin outright if

He had wished. In a thousand ways He could have restored man to his pristine condition. But He chose to draw good out of evil, to demand infinite justice and exhibit infinite mercy, and to give to man the power to attain an even higher station than was his before the fall.

For, by the redemption, the Son of God became man, offered as God-man an infinite reparation for man's offence, showed infinite mercy by His passion and death, and obtained for men of good will the opportunity to become the children of God. "To as many as received Him He gave the power to become the children of God." It was Jesus Christ Himself who taught us to say to the Lord God of heaven and earth: "Our Father, who art in heaven."

CHAPTER V.

The Mother of God

THE Son of God in becoming man had to have a mother. Mary was His mother. The blood which flowed in His veins and which He shed on Calvary was derived from her. It was she who held Him to her breast as a child and cared for Him as a boy. Of all human beings, she was the closest to Him in birth, in life, and in death. Of the millions and millions of women since creation, she was chosen as His mother. Jesus Christ, who was born of her, was both God and man. As God He had no beginning, no birth. As man He was born at a certain time and place. Since His divinity and humanity were united in the one person, Jesus Christ, and since we cannot separate the divinity from Jesus Christ, it follows that the mother of Jesus Christ is also the mother of God.

Sometimes non-Catholics assert that we pay too much honor to Mary. Well, if we do, God has set us the example. If you trust your money to a man, you honor him, but if you trust your child to him, you give him the highest mark of your regard. God chose Mary not merely as the custodian, but as the mother of His Son.

Moreover, He declared her singularly blessed. The Archangel Gabriel bore a message direct from God to her, and, as the ambassador of heaven, saluted her thus: "Hail, full of grace, the Lord is with thee, blessed art thou among women." This angelic messenger bows down before a maiden. Never before had an angel thus shown obeisance to a mortal. He waits on her word. In other cases where God's messengers appeared to mortals, it was to command, but not so in regard to Mary. He salutes her, praises her, delivers his message and then before proceeding awaits her decision. When she finally gave her consent to the mystery, he declared that the Holy One who was to be born of her was to be the Son of God.

The Church of Christ has always revered Mary as the mother of God, imitating in this God Himself, whose messenger Gabriel declared that the Holy One who was to be born of her was to be the Son of God. But, though she is the mother of God, she is not divine. She is, like us, a creature. That is why we love her so much,—she is one of us.

There is an infinite distance between her and God, but nevertheless she is closer to Him than any other created being. And since we know that God honors those who are dear to Him, and since it is His grace that makes us dear to Him, and since His ambassador Gabriel declared her to be full of grace, we know that she is the recipient of all the favor that God can bestow upon a creature.

If God told those who besought His help and forgiveness to go to His friend Job to have him intercede for them, with much more confidence can we go to His mother. And we do.

CHAPTER VI.

The Head of the Church

EVERYTHING has a head,—the family, the city, the state. The bigger a thing and the more widespread and diversified it is, the more need there is of a head. The biggest thing in the world is the Catholic Church, the most widespread thing in the world is the Catholic Church, the most diversified thing in the world is the Catholic Church. The Catholic Church has a head.

We may judge of the kind of head an organization should have by the nature of its activities and constitution. The Catholic Church is active in every part of the world, among every nation and race. The purpose of its activities is to continue among mankind the work begun and established by Jesus Christ. Christ's commission to His Church was: "As the Father hath sent me, so I send you." The Church, therefore, is Christ's continuation in the world, and the head of the Church is His personal representative. For that reason, the Pope is called the Vicar of Christ.

Now it is evident that Jesus Christ, who gave His life to establish His religion, was concerned about its continuance, and its continuance as the pillar and ground of truth. Jesus was the Light of the World. His Church must be the same. Jesus therefore took good care to guarantee the life and the truth of His Church.

When the framers of our country's Constitution finished their work, they did not leave it to itself, but appointed the Supreme Court of the United States as its guardian and interpreter. As far as was in their power, they made the Supreme Court infallible. To uphold its judgments the whole power of the government will be employed. They therefore endowed it with practical infallibility. And why? To insure the integrity and continuance of the Constitution. If men employ every means in their power for the perpetuation of their work, can we imagine that God left His great work to itself to drift along unguided and unprotected!

So even if we did not have His very guarantee that He would be with His Church and safeguard it, we should know anyway that He would provide that

His representative among men would represent Him, and not misrepresent Him.

But we have His actual guarantee. "Thou art Peter, and upon this rock I will build my church, and the gates of hell shall not prevail against it." "The spirit of truth will abide with you forever." "Behold I am with you all days to the end of the world." "Going therefore, teach ye all nations." "I will ask the Father and He shall give you another Paraclete, that He may abide with you forever, the Spirit of Truth." These guarantees were given to the Church by One who had the power to carry them into effect.

Now Peter is the head of the Church. Peter was made head of the Church by its founder, Christ. Our Lord conferred this office on him after his noble profession of faith, in which he declared that Jesus was God: "Thou art Christ, the Son of the Living God." In return, Christ declared: "Thou art Peter [Peter means a rock], and upon thee I will build my church. . . . And I will give to thee the keys of the kingdom of heaven."

What power to confer on a man! The Church is the kingdom of heaven, and to Peter were intrusted the keys. It is to the master, to the head of an establishment, that the keys are intrusted. In all languages, the keys are the symbol of authority and headship. And to show that it was real power Jesus was giving to Peter, He announced: "Whatsoever thou shalt bind upon earth will be bound also in heaven." This was personal to Peter, different from the promises which Christ made to the apostles or the Church at large. He said: "*Thou* art the rock," and "to *thee* will I give the keys," and "whatsoever *thou* shalt bind." Therefore Christ made Peter the head.

After the resurrection, Jesus solemnly confirmed Peter's headship over the Church when He made him shepherd of the flock: "Feed my lambs, feed my sheep." The flock is the body of the faithful, the lambs and sheep represent the people and pastors. Over all these, the head is the shepherd. Christ, the Good Shepherd, on ascending into heaven, constituted Peter shepherd in His place. As Christ was head, so was Peter, and so is the successor of Peter.

The head of the Church, therefore, is the spokesman for this organization to which God guaranteed that the truth should abide with it forever. In virtue of His guarantee, and not for any personal worth of the actual head, God is bound to see to it that the spokesman of His Church, when speaking officially, should never teach error.

Christ said: "Thou art Peter, and upon thee will I build my church." If the foundation, the rock, is not secure, how will the superstructure stand? If the head of the body be insecure, how will the body itself be safe? It is as easy for Christ to guarantee personal infallibility to the head as corporate infallibility to the body. Numbers do not count as an argument or a guarantee. The wisest and most learned assemblies have erred. But he whom God guarantees against error is indeed safe from it.

The Pope personally may or may not be a good man, but officially he is God's Vicar, and as such he cannot mislead the flock intrusted to him. "Feed my lambs, feed my sheep," said Christ to the head of His Church. As God's shepherd, the Pope has God's protection. It is God's business to see to it that His own flock, fed by a shepherd of His own appointment, should receive the food of truth, and not the husks of error.

Hence our security as Catholics, once the Pope has officially spoken. We know it is God's voice. We feel like a child who at a distance hears over the wire his father's voice. The quality of the instrument does not matter, only the voice of the father.

But it is the glory of the Church that her head has been, with a very few exceptions, worthy of his high office. There was a Judas among the twelve under the very eyes of the Master. We should not be surprised if, during twenty centuries, a few, a very few, of the successors of Peter did not live up to their lofty station. But taking them as a body, it is universally conceded that they are the glory of mankind. No dynasty can point to such a noble line of rulers.

In our own day, we can recall Pius IX and Leo XIII and Pius X. This world has seldom seen such a trio of men. All through the centuries the popes have been the true friends of mankind, but especially have they held up to the world the light of truth. They have been persecuted and misrepresented, as was their Master. They do not expect better treatment than was accorded Him. And like Him they will triumph even if it be by death. A Pope dies, but the papacy lives on. God has said it.

CHAPTER VII.

THE BIBLE

THERE is a great deal of misconception about the Bible. Some people think that, in some way or other, it came to us just as it is from heaven. Others think that it was written by God Himself. Again some believe that it existed previous to the Church and that the Church rests on it as upon a foundation.

The Bible means a collection of books or volumes. Far from being the foundation of the Church, it was the Church that collected these volumes together and gave them to us as the Bible. Why, then, you may ask, have I been quoting the Bible all along to substantiate the divinity of Christ and the Church? In so quoting, I was using the Bible as an authentic historical document, not as an inspired record. There are many historical documents which are not the Bible. They have their value just as any true document has. In that sense and no other was Scripture appealed to in our demonstration.

But the Bible, as the Church regards it, is more than a historical document, it is an inspired record. Once you admit it is inspired, there is no need of arguing about the divinity of Christ or the Church, for that is plainly stated in the Bible, which, if inspired, is its own proof. We showed from a historical and critical investigation that the Christian foundation is true. The Catholic argument does not depend at all on the Bible as an inspired book.

But the Bible does depend upon the Church for its genuineness as an inspired record. Ask the average Protestant where the Bible comes from. Perhaps he never thought of that. Well, it was the Catholic Church that, so to speak, made the Bible. That is, she gathered together the different parts, sifted the genuine from the spurious, and then by her authority declared which was the inspired Scripture.

There was no Bible in Christ's time, none in the apostles' time. It came later when the Church, seeing that the inspired letters of the apostles to the various churches, and the gospels written by the inspired evangelists were being tampered with, and spurious ones foisted on the people, examined all the writings claiming to be sacred and designated those as inspired which had as authors the apostles, evangelists, and prophets. These she put together in one collection and called it the Bible. That is the Bible.

The infallible and authoritative Church gave it to us. The infallible and authoritative Church existed before the Bible, and independent of it, and, after giving it to us, safeguarded it down through all the ages.

Protestantism, with its platform of the Bible, and the Bible only, has now virtually discarded the Bible as the inspired word of God. On the other hand, the Catholic Church, which was abused for its lack of appreciation of the Bible, is now its sole upholder and protector as an inspired record. Protestants call it the word of God, but their leading teachers treat it as the word of a human moralist, accepting some parts, discarding others. If they considered it inspired, they would not dare tamper with it as they do.

The Catholic Church is consistent. It gave it to us as the inspired word of God, and it holds it as such. It realizes that on account of its sacredness and sublimity it needs official explanation when there is question as to its meaning.

We do not trust the interpretation of the Constitution of the United States to an individual, no matter how learned he may be. If a question arises as to its meaning, there is but one authoritative declaration, and that is by the Supreme Court. The Bible may be considered the Constitution of the world-wide Catholic Church. Why should an individual take liberties with it, which he cannot take with a human document? The Church alone, the Voice of God, may, in case of doubt, declare truly the meaning of the Bible. Why should not she who, in collecting the material of the Bible, discriminated between the true and the false, not also decide what is the true or false meaning of a particular passage?

Protestants began by individual interpretation, and they are now concluding by wholesale rejection. The Reformers rejected whole chapters if it suited their purpose. To-day their descendants reject doctrine after doctrine according to their fancy. Suppose we did that with the Constitution of the United States! There would very soon be no law or order. And that is precisely the condition of Protestantism to-day.

Outside the Catholic Church all is chaos. Can we imagine the religion of Jesus Christ being such an assemblage of contradictions? No wonder that intelligent Protestants lament their sad state, and that so many reject all religion in turning away from their own disrupted church.

It is for such souls that these pages are written, in hopes that, seeing the wonderful unity and consistency and perpetuity of the Catholic Church, they may recognize in her the Pillar and Ground of Truth, the bride of Christ, the religion of God.

CHAPTER VIII.

HELL

HELL is a subject not supposed to be even mentioned nowadays. It is considered old-fashioned, crude, brutal. Enlightened people shrink from attributing such a monstrous doctrine to the good God. Refined people shudder at the thought of it.

Well, Jesus Christ was refined, enlightened, merciful, broad-minded, and He taught us there is a hell. Moreover, He died on the cross to keep us out of it. Against the word and death of Jesus Christ, the Son of God, there is no argument. If there is no hell, why was Christ crucified? Why did Christ say: "What doth it profit a man to gain the whole world and lose his soul?" If there is no hell, what do these words of Christ mean: "Depart, ye cursed, into everlasting fire?" Why did Jesus say: "If thy eye scandalize thee, pluck it out, for it is better to go with one eye into the kingdom of heaven than having both eyes to be cast into hell?"

If there is no hell, what is the meaning of the mission of Jesus Christ? If there is no hell, what fools the early Christians were to submit to imprisonment, exile, and death! It is estimated that there are nine millions of martyrs. Were they all deluded? If so, it was for believing Jesus Christ; not their own interpretation of His words, but the official declaration of His divinely constituted tribunal.

Deny hell, deny Jesus Christ. You cannot accept one without the other. We believe in hell only because Jesus declares its existence.

Catholics do not relish hell any more than other people. They are not interested in upholding such a dreadful doctrine. But they do believe that Jesus Christ is God, and if He tells them that there is a hell, they believe it. They do not like hell, but that does not make them deny it. They do not like pestilence or war or famine, yet they do not deny these things. Catholics are opposed to hell in one way,—they do all in their power to keep out of it. And that is what God wants. He made hell so terrible to keep us from offending Him.

Fear is the beginning of wisdom. If a child does not have reverence for his father, he cannot have love for him. And we, unless we reverence the authority of God, cannot have true love for Him. Hell helps us to realize the dreadfulness of despising the authority of God. Even as it is, with the fear of hell to deter us from sin, how many turn their backs on God and live to suit themselves.

If with the fear of hell to keep us from evil the world is nevertheless so wicked, what would it be without this restraint?

But, regardless of what we may reason about it, the fundamental thing is this: Jesus Christ solemnly and repeatedly proclaimed that there is a hell, He was crucified to redeem us from hell, He established His Church to enable us to live in such a way as to avoid hell, and He warns us to lose all, even life itself, rather than incur the punishment of hell.

Moreover, God sends no one to hell. Whoever goes there goes in spite of God's best efforts to keep him out of it. God warns, chastises, threatens, He even makes hell so terrible, to keep us out of it. If any man goes to hell, he goes because he has ignored God and His warnings. "What is there that I ought to do more to my vineyard that I have not done to it?"

CHAPTER IX.

The Sacraments

AS stated in regard to the Redemption, God could have employed various means to accomplish it. He chose to do it by the Incarnation and death of His own divine Son. So, in imparting to mankind the fruits of the Redemption, God could have done it in many ways. But it is not for us to inquire why He did not do it this way or that, but to bow down and reverently accept His graces through the channels He has established.

God could have made angels the ministers of His grace, but He has chosen instead men, weak, sinful men. He uses men as His ministers and the sacraments as the means of conveying His grace to us. The sacraments are certain definite rites instituted by Christ for the conferring of grace.

A sacrament is an outward sign instituted by Jesus Christ to give grace to the soul. Man is made up of an exterior or visible body and an interior or invisible soul. The outward sign of a sacrament corresponds to the material part of man, the interior grace imparted partakes of the nature of the soul.

It may be asked why God employs such instrumentalities for the conferring of His grace. The main reason is His own will. He knows man and has chosen the means He sees fit. But nevertheless we may see in the formality of the sacraments very good reasons why they are employed.

As regards the outward sign, it indicates in a fitting way the character of what is imparted to the soul. We know that smoke is a sign of fire, even though we do not see the flames; a sad face is a sign of a heavy heart; black clothes denote mourning; etc., etc. So in the sacraments, water in baptism denotes the washing away of sin; the holy oil in extreme unction indicates the comfort and strength God's grace gives to the parting soul.

It is highly proper that the Church of Christ, which is an outward and visible institution, should dispense God's graces by outward and visible means. Moreover, unless there were an exterior form accompanying the grace of the different sacraments, we should never know for certain that we had received that particular grace. As it is, we have God's word for it that if we do our part, His grace is imparted to us infallibly with the administration of the particular sacrament we receive. We know that we receive the special grace of that particular sacrament when it is administered.

We are sinners, and most of our sins are committed by the instrumentality of our senses. Through these same senses we receive the assurance of God's forgiveness once we have repented and resolved to live rightly.

The Church was established for men, not angels. All her ceremonies are calculated to reach man as he is, a creation of body as well as soul. It thus elevates the whole man, and even here below begins that process by which eventually we become the children of God.

Our Father, who art in heaven, hallowed be thy name: thy kingdom come!

CHAPTER X.

The Eucharist

THE Eucharist is a mystery as well as a sacrament. Like the Trinity and the Incarnation, it is something that surpasses human understanding. We believe it, not because we comprehend it, but simply on God's word, just as we believe in the Trinity and the Incarnation. Our religion is called our holy Faith, because it is based on faith in God's statements. In the Eucharist, we have to trust absolutely to God's word. There is nothing in the Eucharist itself to help our understanding of it, rather everything to make it harder of comprehension. Jesus understood all this, and for that reason prepared His followers for absolute trust in Him.

The Eucharist is the sacrament of the body and blood of Christ. It was instituted Jesus at the Last Supper, when He changed the substance of the bread and wine into His body and blood, and gave Himself to the apostles as their first Holy Communion.

How it is that without any external change there is a change of the real interior substance of the bread into the body of Christ we do not know. Nor does God want us to know. If He did, He would have told us. It is as if, before giving us the greatest thing in His possession, Himself, He demanded this act of perfect faith in Himself. Perfect faith it surely is, for there is nothing but His word for it. However, Christ prepared His followers for this great confidence in Him, as we shall see.

His first miracle was to change water into wine by a mere expression of His will. Afterwards He fed a great multitude of thousands of people with a few loaves. Taking bread into His hands, He blessed it, causing it to increase a thousand-fold before the very eyes of the people. After this miracle, they wished to make Him their king. Taking occasion of their great confidence in Him, He told them that He was going to give them bread of another kind, bread from heaven. When they asked for that bread, He said: "The bread that I will give is my flesh, for the life of the world."

When the people heard this statement they were amazed, and said one to another: "How can He give us His flesh to eat?'" They understood Jesus literally. Had they misunderstood Him? No, for if they had, He would have rightly informed them. But when He saw their astonishment, He repeated and emphasized what He had said: "Amen, amen, I say unto you, except you eat the flesh of the Son of Man and drink of His blood, you shall not have life in you. For my flesh is meat indeed, and my blood is drink indeed."

He held to His statement, although it caused many to turn away from Him. Even some of His disciples left Him. This made Jesus turn towards the apostles and say: "Will you too leave me?" Peter answered: "Lord, if we leave Thee, to whom shall we go? Thou hast the words of eternal life!"

A few days after Christ had raised Lazarus from the dead, on the day before His crucifixion, while seated with His apostles at the Last Supper, Jesus fulfilled His promise of giving to them His body and blood. Taking bread into His hands, He blessed it, saying: "Take ye and eat, this is my body." These words were His last will and testament. Continuing, He said: "Do this for a commemoration of me."

Here was the act of consecration, the changing of the bread into His body, and also the commission to the apostles to do the same, in memory of Him. That this was the way in which the apostles understood it is clear from their practice. St. Paul, speaking of the Eucharist, says: "The bread which we break is it not the partaking of the body of the Lord?" Now, if anyone knew the meaning of the words of our Lord, it was the apostles. It is not likely that Christ allowed them to be deceived.

For fear there may be any question at all as to how they regarded the Eucharist, the Apostle furthermore adds: "He that eateth and drinketh unworthily eateth and drinketh judgment to himself, not discerning the body of the Lord." If words have any meaning at all, these of Christ and the Apostle signify that the Eucharist is the body and blood of Jesus Christ.

Nothing can explain this wonderful mystery. However, it is possible to advert to some things around us which may make our minds more ready to assent to it. Suppose someone told you that a woman could give her flesh and blood as food to another. At first you would say no. But observe. A mother gives her flesh and blood to her nursing child. How? Her substance in some mysterious way is changed into milk. How, not even she knows, nor all the learned men of the world. This milk, her flesh and blood, she gives to her child.

What a mother does indirectly through the medium of milk, God does by the Eucharist. It is for us to adore God for His kindly dispensations in our regard and to thank Him. If we do this not merely by words but by a good life, we shall understand in heaven not only the Eucharist, but all other things. "Eye hath not seen nor ear heard nor hath it entered into the mind of man to conceive the things God hath prepared for them that love Him."

There is no means in this world so well adapted to enable us to love God as the Eucharist. By frequently receiving our Lord, we become more and more like unto Him, and even in this life we become, in a way, incorporated into the divine family. "To as many as receive Him, He gives the power to become the children of God."

CHAPTER XI.

The Mass

THE mass is the most sacred ceremony of the Catholic religion. It is by the mass that the Blessed Eucharist and the crucifixion are perpetuated. Everything in the Church centres about the adorable sacrifice of the mass. It is for the celebration of the mass that the altar is erected. It is as a habitation for the sacramental Christ that our churches are built, where He dwells to receive the homage of His subjects and to bestow His blessing and Himself. It is for the celebration of the mass that our priests are consecrated. It is for a worthy reception of Christ's body and blood effected by the mass that the sacrament of Penance prepares the faithful.

The mass is the great sacrifice of the new law, offered from the rising of the sun to its going down. It is the clean oblation prefigured by the offering of Melchisedech. The mass enables mankind to offer to God daily and repeatedly what is most acceptable to Him. For it is the offering to the eternal Father of the Only Begotten Son. That is why the mass is so sacred.

Sometimes you hear people say that they do not see the need of going to mass. But you never hear a good Catholic say that, for he knows that he is assisting at a great though unbloody sacrifice.

God commands us to worship Him, to keep holy the Sabbath day. The Church specifies how we shall do so. The mass is the great public act of worship. To be present with the right intention and conduct is all that is necessary. Piety will suggest further devotion. But your mere presence constitutes the act of worship for you. You may not be able to hear the words of the mass, you may not understand them, but God to whom they are addressed hears and understands. The mass is an act of sacrifice and all join in it who are present.

At the great inauguration ceremony at Washington, how many of those present hear the words of the President or understand the details of the function, yet all honor the President by their mere presence. So with the mass. Catholics go to mass to adore and worship God in the way He prescribes. Their mere presence is an act of religion. The priest may be cultured or vulgar, the church clean or dirty, the sermon good or bad, the music devotional or detestable,—it matters not. The offering is the main thing, and the offering is of infinite value,—it is none other than Christ Himself.

The mass is the Last Supper over again, with the additional significance of Calvary. God sees everyone who is there, He knows the effort and sacrifice which at times it costs to attend, He knows that the worshippers are there to honor Him.

God does not need us or our gifts. The world is His and the fulness thereof. But what He does want is our heart. We give Him that when we strive to please Him, when we put ourselves out for His sake, when we suffer for Him who suffered so much for us.

The church is God's throne-room, and the altar His very throne. As a monarch receives in state at specified times, so does the Monarch of the world summon His subjects at intervals to renew their allegiance and to honor Him. By the voice of His herald, the Church, He calls His subjects to His throne-room every Sunday. There they acknowledge His Lordship and offer Him their petitions. There they behold over again the sacrifice of Calvary and see the price that was paid for their redemption.

When they return to their homes, it is as men renewed. They have been in touch with something above this world. They have been with Christ. They go forth into the world again, but they live for something more than the world.

CHAPTER XII.

CONFESSION

ONE of the things that seem to repel non-Catholics is confession. But once they become Catholics and have experienced its marvellous help and comfort, they become its strongest advocates. It is a common remark by those outside the Church that there is no need of confessing sins to a priest; it is better to go straight to God Himself.

Very well, but suppose you wished to see the President of the United States and he referred you to his secretary! It is not a question of what might be or should be, but of what is. Has Christ referred us to the priest in this matter of confession? If so, then the matter is closed. There is no room for discussion.

In point of fact, God has established the sacrament of Penance, and it is the ordinary way He has appointed for the forgiveness of sin. I say the ordinary way, for nothing can stand between God and the sinner who turns to Him with a contrite heart. Where confession is not possible, God does not require it. An act of perfect contrition for sin, with the intention of complying with the ordinary requirements should the opportunity offer, will restore the worst offender to God's friendship.

Why does God require us to obtain His forgiveness through confession to a priest? We do not know. It is His ordination. He is the one offended by sin, and it is His right to say how He will pardon. If you offend another, you have no right to tell him in what way he will pardon you. That is his affair. If an offence against one who is but a man like yourself does not permit of your dictating the manner of reconciliation, how much less does your view count when you have offended the majesty of God?

A sinner should be glad to obtain God's forgiveness on any terms. God has stated His terms. He might with justice punish sin on the spot; He might impose on us as a condition of forgiveness, a journey to a distant place; He might forgive sin only after years of reparation; He might require a year or several years of our life for each sin. But instead He has for His own wise reasons established the sacrament of Penance for the forgiveness of sin.

Here are the very words of Christ: "Receive ye the Holy Ghost; whose sins you shall forgive they are forgiven; whose sins you shall retain they are retained." These words were addressed to the apostles. By them they are clothed with power from God Himself to forgive or retain sin.

We see something similar in the state. The government makes laws. If one breaks the law, one offends against the state. The state itself does not punish or release a prisoner, but clothes her judges with power to hear and decide. Even after a prisoner is convicted, the state sometimes forgives him; but how? Not directly, but indirectly through the governor, to whom the state has given the pardoning power.

If the state confers on an individual the pardoning power, why should not God forgive through another if He sees fit? If confession was not established by God Himself, what man would be bold enough to introduce it among men? If it is hard to accept it now after twenty centuries of established use, how much harder was it in the beginning? Unless God Himself was its author, it never could have got a foothold in the world. But once realizing that it is God's way, we soon discover that after all it is the best way.

How many millions of souls have received helpful advice in confession! How many have been turned aside from the path of evil by the warning they received in confession! How many struggling souls have been aided to victory by the prudent and firm guidance of the priest who could be of no help unless he had known their condition in confession! How many priests have been approached by non-Catholics for advice and comfort because it was known that they could open their hearts to a priest in full confidence, as to God Himself. It is safe to say that legions of souls have fought the good fight and conquered by means of the sacrament of Penance.

God's way is the best way always.

CHAPTER XIII.

Marriage

THE family is the most important factor of the state. If the family dies out, so does the state. Rome is an example. There are other instances nearer home. New England furnishes many. The old stock is fast disappearing instead of increasing. That is nature's judgment on man's violation of her laws. Any attempt at interfering with God's rule of the world is fatal. Now God in His providence ordained that the continuation of the world should be accomplished by the family. Any increase of the human race outside the family produces disorder. Marriage is the basis of the family; hence its importance.

Human nature is human nature. You have to take it as it is. It is very fickle. The family is a most serious proposition. It has duties and responsibilities. Men and women need help to enable them to be constant and true as man and wife. If God blesses their union with children, there is the added duty and charge of parents. To bring up children in the fear and love of God calls for faith, patience, tact, and sacrifice. God understands all this much better than we do.

Hence He instituted the sacrament of matrimony to give stability to the marriage contract and to give parents the aids to discharge their duties in the Christian spirit. Therefore is it that He declares that He Himself is the one who performs the marriage ceremony. "What God hath joined together, let no man put asunder." The priest who officiates at the marriage is only God's agent.

It is God Himself who joins the man and woman together and makes of the two but one,—one inseparable union.

Genesis tells us that "God created man to His own image: to the image of God He created him." Afterwards He said: "It is not good for man to be alone, let us make him a helpmate like unto himself." God Himself presented Eve to Adam, and blessing their union, said: "Increase and multiply and fill the earth." God thus established the marriage state and performed Himself the first marriage.

Scripture adds: "Wherefore shall a man leave father and mother and shall cleave to his wife, and they shall be two in one flesh." Mark that it says two, not three, four, or more. Human passion often mars God's arrangements, but passion violates all laws. It is in order to check and govern passion that Christ made marriage a sacrament, a holy thing, that, being sacred, it would be the more respected. St. Paul, referring to matrimony, says: "This is a great sacrament but I speak in Christ and in the Church." The Apostle calls it a great sacrament. What are we to think of those to-day who regard it as a mere business transaction!

There is but one Church in the world to-day that regards marriage as did Christ and the apostles. If there were no other argument for the divinity of the Catholic Church, that would suffice. For marriage, of all things in the world, offers the greatest field for human wilfulness.

Man's heart is so changeable in its affections that it is constantly seeking a device to remove the barriers of restraint. All other religions in the world have made concessions to this tendency except the Catholic Church. Truth is always the same; it changes not to suit the times or the passions. The Catholic Church could have held all England in its fold if it were willing to make a concession to Henry VIII on marriage. Can we imagine Christ making compromise with sin? Neither could His representative.

Marriage has as great difficulties for Catholics as it has for Protestants or infidels, but they meet it as God directs, and in the end they are gainers by it. A man and wife may have their differences, but if they know that their union is indissoluble, they patch them up. But if they feel that they can make a new alliance, the breach widens and soon a chasm yawns between them. And what becomes of the children!

Again, if man and wife fear a dissolution of the marriage, they may take precautions against having children. Suppose their fathers and mothers did that, where would they and their children be now! If the thing is lawful, one has as much right to do it as another, and soon where would the world be! So we can readily see that there is need of a powerful influence in the world to keep it from the vagaries and ruin of passion.

There is but one influence on earth to-day that safeguards marriage, and that is the sacrament of matrimony of the Catholic Church. The sex instinct is the strongest human passion. Among every race it is the hardest thing to control and is the source of untold evils.

The Catholic Church alone, as the voice of God, speaks out authoritatively and uncompromisingly on this matter. If she were not divine, she could not have the courage to stand up before the tide of sensuality that has swept aside every other barrier. By her lofty ideals, by her examples of virginity, by her sacraments, and by her perpetual reminder of the judgments of God, she gives man a power to rise superior to the baseness within him.

Mankind should welcome an institution which makes the family secure, brings respect to father and mother, and safeguards the virtue of son and daughter.

CHAPTER XIV.

Prayer

SOME people think that prayer is only a petition, a request for something. This is but one form of prayer and perhaps the lowest. The "Our Father," which is an ideal prayer, shows us that prayer is an act of praise as well as of petition. It begins by an act of praise: "Our Father, who art in heaven, hallowed be thy name." Besides, prayer is also an act of thanksgiving for God's favors and also an act of reparation for our offences.

Prayer holds a very important place in the true Church. The good Catholic begins and ends the day with prayer. In the hour of temptation he seeks strength in prayer. When in sorrow, prayer is his solace; when in joy, it is his thanksgiving.

The great official prayer of the Church is the mass. This prayer every Catholic joins in as a matter of obligation on Sundays and holydays. By the mass there is offered to God praise, thanksgiving, reparation, and petition. It is an act of worship that fulfils all the purposes of prayer. If a man does not attend mass regularly, he virtually ceases to be a Catholic. Of course he is a Catholic in name, but he is cutting himself off from the greatest source of grace which his religion affords. Moreover, he is, as it were, turning his back on God, for he refuses to give Him the service He commands.

If a subject refuses to appear at a state function when ordered by his sovereign, he falls into disfavor. God commands us under pain of sin to honor Him once a week by attendance at mass. Not to do so is to despise His authority and to incur His displeasure. Of course if one is not able to go to mass, there is no obligation. Any serious inconvenience, one, say, that would keep a person from business, is a sufficient reason for not attending mass. But to deliberately stay away from mass on Sunday simply because you want to rest, or read, or recreate, is to ignore the ordinance of God and is an act of disobedience to Him.

A man who calls himself a Catholic and neglects mass on Sunday is like a soldier who would stay at home when ordered to the ranks. We know what would happen to the soldier. The majesty of God is greater than that of any earthly ruler, and He, in His own time and way, will know how to requite those who ignore Him.

Besides this great and obligatory prayer of the mass, there are the morning and evening prayers. A prayer is the uplifting of the mind to God or His saints. By beginning the day with a reminder of God above, we go forth strengthened for the trials and temptations inseparable from life. In the same way, at the close of the day before retiring for the night, we again raise our minds to heaven, our true home, to thank God for His goodness and to beg pardon for our transgressions and shortcomings.

In this way, the faithful Catholic is in constant touch with the supernatural. He realizes that although he must live in this world, he is not living merely for it, but also and mainly for that blessed life beyond where there is true peace and joy. This thought enables him to meet the burden of the day and to discharge his duty cheerfully. For he knows that the reward hereafter depends on the fidelity with which his duty is performed here. And so he goes ahead serving God gladly, doing his duty by his fellow-man, and striving in all things to make himself worthy of companionship with the children of God in heaven.

This life is only the first step of our existence. The longest life seems at its close but brief. What matters it if the short path which leads to our Father's home be steep and rugged if only it leads us securely to Him! On the other hand, if the path of this life leads us away from God, "What doth it profit a man if he gain the whole world and lose his soul?" God established His Church and the sacraments to guide and help us in the way that leads to Himself.

"Thy kingdom come, O Lord, Thy will be done on earth as it is in heaven! May Thy will be done by me! May Thy kingdom come to me!"

A LIST OF BOOKS

WHICH GO DEEPER INTO THE QUESTIONS HERE TOUCHED UPON

THE CATHOLIC ENCYCLOPEDIA
THE FAITH OF OUR FATHERS, *Cardinal Gibbons.*
WHO AND WHAT IS CHRIST? *F. Roh, S.J.*
THE EXISTENCE OF GOD, *R. F. Clarke, S.J.*
CHURCH OR BIBLE, *Arnold Damen, S.J.*
PLAIN FACTS FOR FAIR MINDS, *G. M. Searle, C.S.P.*
THE QUESTION BOX, *B. L. Conway, C.S.P.*
CATHOLIC BELIEF, *Di Bruno.*
EVIDENCES OF RELIGION, *James L. Balmes.*
HANDBOOK OF THE CHRISTIAN RELIGION, *Wilmers, S.J.*
THE OLD RIDDLE AND THE NEWEST ANSWER, *John Gerard, S.J.*

SCIENCE

THE CHURCH AND SCIENCE, *Sir Bertram Windle, F.R.S., F.S.A.*

HISTORY

EUROPEAN CIVILIZATION, *James L. Balmes.*
ENGLAND, *John Lingard.*
LOLLARDY AND THE REFORMATION, *James Gairdner.*
PER CRUCEM AD LUCEM, *T. W. Allies.*
THE EVE OF THE REFORMATION, *Cardinal Gasquet.*
HENRY VIII AND THE ENGLISH MONASTERIES, *Cardinal Gasquet.*
BREAKING WITH THE PAST, *Cardinal Gasquet.*
THE OLD ENGLISH BIBLE, *Cardinal Gasquet.*
THE POPES, *Hartmann Grisar, S.J.*
LUTHER, *Hartmann Grisar, S.J.*

www.ingramcontent.com/pod-product-compliance
Lightning Source LLC
Chambersburg PA
CBHW051928110726
47902CB00002B/463